FOUNDATIONS OF MODERN ECONOMICS SERIES

RICHARD T. GILL *Harvard University*

Evolution
of Modern Economics

PRENTICE-HALL, INC. *Englewood Cliffs, New Jersey*

PRENTICE-HALL FOUNDATIONS
OF MODERN ECONOMICS SERIES

Otto Eckstein, *Editor*

Current printing (last digit):
10 9 8 7 6 5 4 3 2 1

PRENTICE-HALL INTERNATIONAL INC., *London*
PRENTICE-HALL OF AUSTRALIA, PTY., LTD., *Sydney*
PRENTICE-HALL OF CANADA, LTD., *Toronto*
PRENTICE-HALL OF INDIA PVT. LTD., *New Delhi*
PRENTICE-HALL OF JAPAN, INC., *Tokyo*

C

Foundations

of Modern Economics Series

Economics has grown so rapidly in recent years, it has increased so much in scope and depth, and the new dominance of the empirical approach has so transformed its character, that no one book can do it justice today. To fill this need, the Foundations of Modern Economics Series was conceived. The Series, brief books written by leading specialists, reflects the structure, content, and key scientific and policy issues of each field. Used in combination, the Series provides the material for the basic one-year college course. The analytical core of economics is presented in *Prices and Markets* and *National Income Analysis,* which are basic to the various fields of application. *Prices and Markets,* a new book prepared especially for this edition of the Series, takes the beginning student through the elements of that subject step-by-step. *The Price System* is a more sophisticated alternative carried over from the first edition. Two books in the Series, *The Evolution of Modern Economics* and *Economic Development: Past and Present,* can be read without prerequisite and can serve as an introduction to the subject.

The Foundations approach enables an instructor to devise his own course curriculum rather than to follow the format of the traditional textbook. Once analytical principles have been mastered, many sequences of topics can be arranged and specific areas can be explored at length. An instructor not interested in a complete survey course can omit some books and concentrate on a detailed study of a few fields. One-semester courses stressing either macro-

v

or micro-economics can be readily devised. The instructors guide to the Series indicates the variety of ways the books in the Series can be used.

This Series is an experiment in teaching. The positive response to the first edition has encouraged us to continue, and to develop and improve, the approach. The thoughtful reactions of many teachers who have used the books in the past have been of immense help in preparing the second edition —in improving the integration of the Series, in smoothing some rough spots in exposition, and in suggesting additional topics for coverage.

The books do not offer settled conclusions. They introduce the central problems of each field and indicate how economic analysis enables the reader to think more intelligently about them, to make him a more thoughtful citizen, and to encourage him to pursue the subject further.

Otto Eckstein, *Editor*

Contents

The problems and methods of economics are ever changing. In the 1960's economists speak of rapid economic growth and the concerns of an affluent society; thirty years ago the great issues were depression and economic stagnation; a hundred and fifty years ago a central worry was the possibility that the working classes might reproduce themselves so rapidly that they would remain forever at the "subsistence" level. Over still longer periods, the changes are even greater. Five hundred years ago, the field of economics could hardly be said to exist except as a rather obscure branch of moral philosophy or theology. Today, it is a complex, professional discipline, an indispensable guide to citizen and State, an important avenue by which men approach the analysis of human society.

How and why such changes have occurred is the subject of this book. It is the story of the evolution of a major modern intellectual discipline, and, since this discipline happens to be a social science, it is also a partial record of man's changing attitudes toward himself and his fellows.

The main themes of this evolution can be caught in two contrasting adjectives—*cumulative* and *controversial*. From the beginning, economists have had aspirations toward the scientific. In the late seventeenth century, the English physician, Sir William Petty, wrote his *Discourses on Political Arithmetic* with the object of dealing with economic phenomena in terms of "Number, Weight, or Measure." In the next century, economists were searching for

1

the "natural laws" which governed the social universe much as the Newtonian laws were thought to govern the physical universe. Economists have not always succeeded in their emulation of the natural scientists, but the effort to do so has had its effect on the development of the field. In particular, it has given that development a *cumulative* quality. Each generation has corrected inconsistencies in the work of the preceding generation and has brought new generality to the theoretical structure or a closer correspondence to observed reality. For this reason, we can speak of a certain mainstream development of economic analysis over the past two or three centuries in which the later work replaces the earlier not as a matter of taste but simply because it is better economics—more consistent, general, and realistic.

But economics is not a pure science; it is impure, uncertain, and *controversial.* No one in the modern world can fail to see that economists often differ; indeed, the Cold War divides the present-day world into two (really more than two) camps in part because of differences about what is or is not valid economics. Throughout the history of the field there have been important critics of the mainstream—men like Karl Marx or our own Thorstein Veblen—who have sought to challenge and overthrow the accepted systems of thought and replace them with their own particular versions of what economic reality truly is.

These critics are actually very important for an understanding of the evolution of modern economics. In some cases (as in the obvious case of Marx) they still exert great influence today; in other cases, their criticisms have not been fully answered and the issues they raised must be resolved by the future progress of the field. Most important of all perhaps, their critical analysis of standard economic doctrine brings out the vital and sometimes hidden assumptions on which that doctrine is based.

And, indeed, this is a significant aspect of the whole study of the history of economic ideas. Any student who reads only the current version of mainstream economics will miss much of what is assumed beneath the surface. How can these basic assumptions be brought vividly to light? By showing how they have developed cumulatively over time and how they have been subject to the controversy of the critics. Only in this way does modern economics gain the depth, the light and shadow, of the major intellectual discipline it is.

EARLY ANTICIPATIONS

When then did it all begin? When was what we call the field of economics born?

In one sense, economics begins with the historical record of human society since all societies have faced economic problems and there have always been philosophers, scribes, prophets, and statesmen to ponder these problems and comment on them. In another sense, we could if we wished ignore everything before about the middle of the eighteenth century, for it is only then that economics, as the separate and systematic discipline we know today, begins to emerge.

A safe generalization is that progress in economic analysis in the pre-modern period was quite slow. The ancient Greeks are a partial exception. They gave us the term "economics" from the words οἴκου (house) and νόμος (rule), or, essentially, household management. They left commentaries on a number of economic problems such as Plato's analysis of division of labor in the *Republic* or Xenophon's treatise on the revenues of Athens. They can even be credited with producing the first economist in the person of Aristotle (384-322 B.C.) since the great philosopher penetrated beneath the surface in his writings on money, exchange, and value. Still, even in the case of the Greeks, progress was fairly slow and their contribution to economics cannot be compared with the much richer gifts they left to such fields as political theory, ethics, logic, science, and art.

With the decline of Greek civilization, further development falters. The Romans did very little in the way of analytic economics and produced no figure in the field who could be compared with Aristotle. In the Middle Ages, progress continues to be halting, although there is the important work of St. Thomas Aquinas (1225?-1274) to be noticed. Economics at this time was very much dominated by the larger social and religious issues that played such a great role in the psychology of medieval life generally. Thus, the characteristic medieval concern was with such issues as "just price" or the propriety of "usury." "To sell a thing for more than its worth, or to buy it for less than its worth, is in itself unjust and unlawful," St. Thomas wrote in his *Summa Theologica*. Or again: "It is by its very nature unlawful to take payment for the use of money lent." These quotations catch the flavor of much medieval economic writing; the interest in how men should behave and how that behavior can be related to a larger conception of society was keener than the more matter-of-fact question of how men actually do behave in the day-to-day business of life.

That economics should have been so long in establishing its own separate and special domain is not so very surprising. Man's behavior in the economic sphere is simply an aspect of his behavior generally, and the natural thing is to view this behavior as a totality. It takes a special and intellectually difficult effort to detach economic considerations from the host of other human considerations with which they seem hopelessly intertwined. But we also must not overlook the importance of economic *conditions* and their influence on the development of the field. The fact is that economic life in pre-modern society was on the whole vastly different from what we are accustomed to. The pace of change was much less rapid and the structure of economic institutions was less complex and much more subject to the governance of accepted, traditional practices. The economic life of the **3** medieval serf tilling the fields with his crude implements was very hard, but it was not particularly complicated. In such a world, it was very easy to take the economic system as given; the need for detailed analysis was far from compelling.

MODERN BEGINNINGS
—THE MERCANTILISTS

But then the need did become compelling. The sixteenth and seventeenth centuries found important new currents stirring in European life. This was the age of the great discoveries, of the commercial revolution, of the mercantile and colonial rivalries between the countries of Europe. It was also the age of the growth of centralized states out of the more fragmented political structure of medieval life. Statesmen began to seek ways of utilizing economic forces to fortify governments at home and secure advantages over rivals abroad.

The writers who dealt with economic issues at this time are usually called *mercantilists,* although they formed no unified group and came from all different walks of life. They included merchants, like the Englishman Sir Thomas Mun (1571-1641), who served on the board of the East India Company; government officials, like Jean Baptiste Colbert (1619-1683), the great French Finance Minister; pamphleteers, like the Austrian Philipp Wilhelm von Hornick (1638-1712), whose nationalistic pamphlet—"Austria Over All If She Only Will"—went through twelve editions. The common bond of most of these men was that, unlike their medieval predecessors, they took a rather this-worldly view of the economic forces they saw operating around them; also, they had a keen feel for the national and political implications of economic policies.

The interpenetration of economic and political considerations can, indeed, be seen in all the characteristic themes of mercantilist writing. With few exceptions, these themes included:

First, a conviction that state intervention is necessary for the proper management of society's economic affairs. One economic historian has described England in the heyday of the mercantilists as experiencing her first "planned economy." [1] Actually, mercantilist statesmen did not automatically approve all acts of intervention in the private economy; some of their most important efforts were directed toward removing artificial barriers to free trade within their national boundaries. But they did take it for granted that the economic interests of the different members and classes of society could and often did come into conflict and, in such circumstances, they felt, the state must take a governing role.

[1] E. Lipson in his *Planned Economy or Free Enterprise* (London: Adam and Charles Black, 1946). The standard reference for a full discussion of mercantilism is Eli Heckscher, *Mercantilism* (London: Allen & Unwin, 1935).

Second, they argued that money, usually in the form of precious metals or treasure, had an important part to play in determining the economic well-being of the nation. The mercantilist position (or really positions) about money and its role in the economy has been subject to many interpretations. It has been said that they grossly confused money and wealth. It has been said that the political motive was strong, treasure being of great importance to the sovereign for such national objectives as raising navies or waging war. They have also been credited with anticipating a rather sophisticated view of money that became current only in our own century. We shall be touching on some of these points again later on, but it is worthwhile noting here that this question of the role of money in the economy—raised so actively by the mercantilists—is one of the important questions that runs through the whole evolution of our subject.

Third, and largely in consequence of the above, they believed that state intervention was necessary to promote a "favorable balance of trade" (roughly, an excess of exports over imports) and thus an inflow of gold and silver. This is perhaps the most well-known mercantilist doctrine and it also touches on an issue, free versus regulated trade, that surges through the entire history of economics. Mercantilist doctrine was not at all uniform on this point, much depending on the sophistication of the particular writer. There does, however, occur in much mercantilist thinking the assumption that a favorable balance is the main and perhaps *only* gain from international trade, as though trade that balances simply cancels out. This assumption was to be sharply challenged by economists in the next period.

Because mercantilist economics was very much infused with political considerations, because much of it was pamphleteering and tract-writing on particular issues of the moment, because the writers themselves were actively engaged in the world of affairs and could not give the subject the time or depth of consideration it ultimately requires—for these various reasons, the mercantilists did not leave behind a structure of systematic economic analysis which later economists could take as their point of departure. Consequently, they are better viewed as forerunners than as founders of modern economics. Still, their contribution was a highly significant one. They brought economic questions to the fore with a sharpness, an urgency, and a realism that had been lacking in earlier times. Furthermore, their views have shown a great deal of vitality over the succeeding centuries, particularly in the area of public policy. All statesmen, to this day, seem to have something of the "mercantilist" in them. If mercantilism was soon to be discredited in the eyes of the new economists, it was far from losing the day completely in the world of actual practice.

A NOTE ON THE PHYSIOCRATS

One other group of forerunners should be noted in passing. Indeed, some would say that this group should be treated as founders since their work has a systematic quality the mercantilists lacked. The group was the *physiocrats* who wrote in France in the third quarter of the eighteenth century; their leading member was François Quesnay (1694-1774) who was court physician to Louis XV and Madame de Pompadour; and their great creation was Quesnay's *Tableau Économique,* in which economic life was rendered as a series of quantitative flows between the different sectors of the economy.

Physiocratic thought was not without its flaws. It was economics of the pre-Industrial Revolution era and this shows clearly in the heavy emphasis the physiocrats placed on agriculture ("productive Expenditures") above industry and trade ("sterile Expenses"). Still, the *Tableau* was a quite remarkable performance, showing an awareness of the interdependence of the different elements of an economic system. The problem of interdependence is a pivotal one for modern economics and the physiocrats can be said to have anticipated, at least in a spiritual sense, the general equilibrium theorists of the late nineteenth century and even the input-output practitioners of the present day.[2]

They also had a more immediate effect. They developed the concept of natural laws into that of a natural order of society ("physiocracy" means "rule of nature"). Quesnay argued that the laws of the physical universe operate as advantageously as possible for human beings, that human beings should morally conform to these advantageous laws, and that, when the social order was properly reformed, the result would be an harmonious society guaranteeing maximum satisfaction for all. For the moment, such a program meant an active role for the state. The French economy of Quesnay's day was bound up in a great legacy of feudalistic and mercantilistic restrictions, and he believed that the absolute monarch should institute modernizing reforms. In the long run, however, the essential feature of his natural order of society was that the state would *not* practice active intervention, that the pursuit of each individual's self-interest would *itself* lead to the best interest of all.

This is a doctrine of natural harmony quite different from the characteristic mercantilistic approach. And it is a doctrine of great historical interest. For it was in connection with the view of economic life as individualistic, self-regulating, and essentially harmonious—the view that recommended *laissez-faire* for the state and the pursuit of self-interest for the individual—that systematic economic analysis made its first definitive appearance on the world scene. When Adam Smith's great *Wealth of Nations* was published in 1776, the ground was already well-prepared!

6

[2] For our discussion of general equilibrium theory see Chapter 4, below. We shall touch only briefly on input-output analysis in our final postscript, p. 105, below.

THE CURTAIN RISES

By the middle of the eighteenth century, then, economics had already had a long history, but, until shortly before, a relatively undeveloped history. From this point onward, however, the pattern changes significantly. Not only is there a great increase in the sheer volume of economic writing; there is also a perceptible change in its quality and purpose. It is no longer enough simply to write a pamphlet on some burning public question. There is now a need to create a system of thought in which the interconnection of apparently unrelated matters is explicitly shown. Threads must be brought together and woven into a fabric. And with this emergence of systematic economics it is also no longer sufficient for the student of economic ideas to gain a vague sense of the opinions of economists. He must participate to some degree in the work of economic analysis. The following pages therefore are not merely description. They will attempt to show not only what views past economists have held but why they have held them and, not least important, how this underlying body of analysis has evolved over time.

Classical Economics

In the year 1776 the economy of the British Isles was in a state of transition. It was in the early stages of the phenomenon known as the Industrial Revolution, which was to transform not only Britain but all the industrial countries of the world into the rapidly growing economies of modern times. For the moment, this transformation lay mainly in the future. But there were a host of other changes that were already fully apparent. Commerce was expanding both internationally and domestically, improvements were taking place in agriculture and industry, population was beginning to grow, complex economic institutions like the banking and credit system were in process of development. Britain was moving rapidly toward a full-fledged "market economy"—an economy in which both commodities and the services of factors of production [1] are regularly offered for sale in the market place and in which production for private profit is the norm.

From the point of view of the development of the field of economics, this growth of a "market economy" in Britain posed a number of challenging questions. Should these private forces be allowed to expand free and unchecked? Or should there be even greater state guidance and regulation (*à la* the mercantilist period) to insure the social welfare and other national objectives? Great

[1] *Factors of production* are the productive agents that are used to make economic goods and services and are often divided into labor, land (or natural resources), and capital. The prices of these factors are their incomes —e.g., wages of labor, rent of land, interest, or sometimes profit, on capital. These concepts will come up many times in the course of this book.

9

issues of public policy clearly hung in the balance. But there was also the intellectual challenge. To show how a private market economy can work, to show how it can grow, to show how, though individualistically organized, it is capable of responding to the needs of society—such questions were rich in content, difficult, fascinating. And with the attempt to answer them, the field of "political economy" begins to separate from the other moral and social disciplines and to enter its new and modern phase.

ADAM SMITH
AND THE "WEALTH OF NATIONS"

The great seminal work in this development was, of course, Adam Smith's *Wealth of Nations* published in that fateful year 1776. Interestingly, the book is not an example of outstanding originality. Smith drank freely of the intellectual currents of his time and, in some respects, was better at coordinating accepted ideas than at initiating new ones. What he did have, however, was weight and scale. He saw the problem of the "market economy" in the round. He saw it intellectually and he saw it in terms of public policy and purpose. Authoritative and persuasive, his work became the foundation of classical economics [2] and set forth the problems that were to occupy most economists for the next century.

His General Approach

In an outward sense, Adam Smith's life was anything but dramatic. He was born in Kirkaldy, Scotland, in 1723, and, at the age of 17, traveled to Oxford where he passed the next 7 years. He was a natural scholar and most of his time at Oxford was spent in the Balliol College library where he read everything he could lay his hands on. After Oxford came a period of lecturing at Edinburgh and then appointment to the Chair of Moral Philosophy at Glasgow. In the years 1764 and 1765 there was some outward drama in

[2] The term "classical economics" has had many different usages among economists. In the 1930's, John Maynard Keynes used the term to cover virtually the entire body of earlier (i.e., pre-Keynesian) economic literature. Professor Schumpeter, in his great posthumously published *History of Economic Analysis,* used "classical" to denote any one of several periods in the development of economic thought when there was fairly general acceptance of certain common economic doctrines. Our usage has an element of Schumpeter's meaning but is limited to a particular period and a particular group of economists. The period is the late eighteenth and early nineteenth century and the economists include such great names as Adam Smith, Thomas Robert Malthus, David Ricardo, and, slightly later, John Stuart Mill. This usage—which, by the way, is probably the most common—conveys the idea that it was during this period and through these men that modern economics received is first systematic treatment and, further, that this treatment was durable in the sense that much subsequent economic thinking can be viewed as a comment upon it or departure from it. Not all experts would accept this view of the matter, but many would and the reasons why they would will become clear in the course of this book.

Smith's life when he took the Grand Tour of the Continent. He went as tutor to the young Duke of Buccleugh, the step-son of Charles Townshend (of our Revolutionary War fame) and had the good fortune to meet Voltaire and to discuss economics with Quesnay. But the following year it was back home again and, for the next decade, he stayed largely in Kirkaldy working on his great treatise. He never married and when he died in 1790, his entire inheritance was to be found in his writings.

This inheritance was a rich one and it was by no means confined to economics. In his early years at Oxford, Smith had become intrigued by the history of science and had composed an essay on the history of astronomy that showed a quite sophisticated sense of the motives which prompt scientific study. (According to Smith, men pursue science not for "any expectation of advantage from its discoveries" but "for its own sake, as an original pleasure or good in itself.") Later on, he wrote an excellent philosophic treatise, *The Theory of Moral Sentiments* (1759), in which he traced the development of man's moral sense to what he called *sympathy,* a term which, for him, meant not simply "pity" or "compassion," but the ability to participate vicariously in the experiences of other people. He wrote at a time when it was still possible to take, if not a comprehensive, at least a very broad view of the different areas of knowledge, and his work outside economics often achieves real distinction.

Even in his masterpiece this same breadth of view is apparent. The *Wealth of Nations* is not the dry, spare, technical treatise that many later writings in economics were to become. It is a spacious, sometimes confusing, often digressive, rich, luxuriant, wide-ranging book. And it is also a pleasure to read, for, despite his digressions and occasional inconsistencies, Smith paid great attention to style and was capable of summing up a major argument in a single sentence or even phrase. "What is prudence in the conduct of every private family can scarce be folly in that of a great Kingdom." "It is not from the benevolence of the butcher, the brewer, or the baker that we expect our dinner, but from their regard to their self-interest." His phrase, "invisible hand," still haunts the corridors of economic thought and has probably been quoted at one time or another by virtually every living economist.

As the title of his book indicates, the problem Adam Smith set himself was to inquire into the nature and causes of the "wealth" of nations. His concept of "wealth" is important because it indicates immediately how he conceived the basic subject matter of economics. He is at great pains to disassociate himself from the "popular notion" (which he attributes somewhat unfairly to the mercantilists) that "wealth consists in money, or in gold or silver." What Smith is concerned with is what economists today would call the *real* economic variables. Smith refers to them as "all the necessaries and conveniences of life" or, alternatively, "the annual produce of the land and labour of the society." He is concerned with goods that can be consumed and invested—wheat, cloth, tools, machines—and the basic factors of production that produce them.

Having taken this step, Smith then goes on to take a *further* step (and here he clearly does conflict with most mercantilist thought) by denying that money has any very special role to play in determining the basic economic health of the nation. As a standard instrument of exchange, money is, of course, a "useful" commodity. Furthermore, since gold and silver are the product of the society's land and labor they are a part of the nation's wealth, but they are a small part, and, indeed, Smith compares money unfavorably with the average commodity. "Goods can serve many other purposes besides purchasing money, but money can serve no other purpose besides purchasing goods." Essentially, one takes money only to get rid of it, to buy goods for consumption, or to invest in productive enterprises.

With such a view, Adam Smith naturally makes short work of the mercantilist argument that the government should intervene actively to secure a favorable balance of trade. What value did Europe gain from the great inflow of gold and silver from the American mines in the sixteenth century? The main result was simply to make the precious metals cheaper (i.e., to raise the prices of all other commodities.) The truly important gains from trade have to do, not with gold and silver, but with the exchange of needed commodities and the widening of markets which may stimulate specialization and more efficient production.

From the beginning, therefore, classical economics was rooted in a *real* or non-monetary view of economic phenonena in this dual sense: the prime subject-matter of economics is the basic stuff of production and consumption and (a much stronger position) the *analysis* of this basic stuff can be undertaken without paying much attention to money, which is primarily a convenient instrument of exchange. With some important exceptions, this approach tended to dominate mainstream economic thought until well into the twentieth century.

Adam Smith's objection to government intervention in foreign trade was not, however, based simply on his views about money. It was rather one part of his general philosophy of economic life which is often called the doctrine of *laissez-faire* and which he sometimes referred to as the "system of natural liberty." It was the articulation of this philosophy and its applicability to the British conditions of the time which more than anything else accounted for the great popular success of Smith's work in his own day.

This doctrine—stated in its essence—is that the state should confine its intervention in economic life to a minimum and that the business of society should be carried on by the interplay of private forces operating through the principle of individual self-interest. Since this doctrine is sometimes misunderstood, a few comments about it are in order:

12   First, this doctrine is in no way simple or obvious. This point needs to be stressed because the underlying idea has so influenced subsequent economic

thought that we are sometimes inclined to treat it as a commonplace. But in fact it is not at all clear why an unregulated market economy subject to the changing decisions (and whims) of countless individuals each operating independently of others should lead to a socially beneficial outcome. Indeed, the *simple* view is that, without some over-all direction and guidance, such an approach would produce economic chaos!

Second, Smith does not take the easy way out by assuming that it is within the self-interest of individuals to promote the welfare of society. He distrusts merchants who profess to trade from motives of public interest and, in truth, he distrusts the business classes generally. "People of the same trade," he writes, "seldom meet together, even for merriment and diversion, but the conversation ends in a conspiracy against the public, or in some contrivance to raise prices." His doctrine clearly does not rest on an assumed spirit of public-mindedness among the citizenry!

Third and finally, although the doctrine urges confining the role of the state to a minimum, it does not deny it any role whatsoever. The sovereign in Smith's view has three main tasks: national defense, the administration of justice, and, more significantly here, the maintenance of certain public works and institutions which it would *not* be in the interest of individuals to maintain but which nevertheless *would* be in the general interest of society. Most notable perhaps is his insistence on the need for public education for the laboring poor who might otherwise be barbarized by the repetitive and mechanical tasks demanded of them by an economically advancing civilization. The point is that the doctrine of the ultimate harmony of private and social interests is seen to have some exceptions; it is not applicable without limit.

Still, the exceptions are relatively few and the applicability very broad. Even in those cases where Smith allows the propriety of governmental intervention it is clear that he would prefer, if it could be so arranged, to have the matter handled privately. The essence of the system of "natural liberty" remains that "every man, as long as he does not violate the laws of justice, is left perfectly free to pursue his own interest his own way." It is this proposition which underlies Smith's characteristic approach to economic phenomena and through the operation of which, he believes, the wealth of nations can best be secured.

The Mechanism of the "Invisible Hand"

But why? By what argument is this not-obvious proposition established? As we have said, it is not only or even primarily the doctrines of great thinkers which interest the student of economic thought but the *analysis* which sustains them.

In the case of Adam Smith's analysis, several elements combined to yield the same general conclusion. One element, for example, had to do with his belief in the greater efficacy of decentralized decision-making. The private individual knows his local situation, knows what products can best be produced

13

there and how best to produce them, is closer to the rewards and punishments of the activity in question. Administration from the central government tends to be too removed, uninformed, and subject to many abuses. For this reason he prefers where possible to rely on local government as opposed to the central government, but better yet on private individuals.

But this in itself is not sufficient, for it must also be shown how these private decisions will be brought into conformity with the interest of society. What is the mechanism by which individuals, who have no object but their own personal gain, are "led by an invisible hand" to promote the welfare of the community? And Smith's answer was that the mechanism was to be found in the market system operating through the forces of competition. In so stating, he was delineating a set of problems which have remained central to modern economics to this day.

The forces of market competition in the Smithian system produce this happy result in two ways: (1) They guarantee that producers will supply the commodities that consumers are demanding and at a price which, in each case, represents the "worth" of the commodity or "what it really costs the person who brings it to market." (2) They guarantee good management in the production of commodities so that these costs are kept low. Competition, in short, guides production into those channels which consumers desire, prevents consumers from being overcharged, and insures them reasonably efficient production.

To have established his position fully, Smith would have needed a more developed analytic apparatus than he actually possessed. Still, he does show a considerable insight into the workings of a competitive market and, in particular, into the ways in which private interest may be transmuted into an agency of social benefit. Suppose, for example, that there is a change in consumer tastes. Suppose that the consuming public develops a sudden fancy for clothing made of cotton cloth. How is this change in preferences registered in an economy activated solely by motives of personal profit?

> In the Smithian world, an increased demand for cotton cloth would show itself in the first instance through an increased competition among the buyers of cotton cloth. This competition would be more or less animated depending on how small the original supply of cotton cloth was and upon the "wealth and wanton luxury" of the competitors. In any event, the result would be a rise in the price of the newly-demanded commodity. That is, the "market price" (the actual price) would rise above the "natural price" (the price just sufficient to cover costs including the going rate of profit). This, in turn, would mean that producers of cotton cloth would be enjoying profits *above* the going rate.
>
> But the process then moves on to the next step. It is in the producers' self-interest to respond to these higher profits. Firms producing cotton cloth will be stimulated by the higher profits to expand production. Firms from other industries, attracted by the higher profits, will join in. And the end-result of *this* part of the process will be: (1) there will be a greater produc-

tion of cotton cloth, which is in accord with consumer demands; and (2) the price of cotton cloth will return to its "natural" level.

In short, the economy has adjusted its productive apparatus to consumer desires—more cotton cloth and at reasonable prices—even though, during the process, no one has given any thought to the consumer, or to society, but has attended solely to his own private interests.

The problem that we have just described may be called the problem of *competitive equilibrium,* and it is one that we shall want to return to again. For the moment, however, we must note that Smith's treatment of the problem was not complete. For one thing, he was hampered by an inadequate theory of value.[3] It was, even in those days, a time-honored question to ask: Why is it that one commodity is cheap and another expensive? Smith rejected the notion that the answer was to be found in the *utilities* of the commodities on the grounds that water is highly useful and cheap and diamonds are much less useful but expensive.[4] He, therefore, sought the answer in the *costs* of producing the commodities, but he did not follow the matter through fully and thus it is unclear what his theory of value was, or whether, properly speaking, he had one.

Furthermore, Smith's analysis, though universal in purpose, is somewhat special in assumption. For it tends to work properly only when there are large numbers of fairly small business firms. As Smith himself says, two grocers are better than one and with twenty grocers the "competition would be just so much greater." The assumption that a private economy would characteristically have large numbers of competing firms was certainly natural enough in an age when the typical scale of business was still small and when it was possible to believe (as Smith did) that the joint-stock company (forerunner of the great modern corporation) did not have much of a future. But, clearly, other assumptions are also possible, and different conclusions result from them.

Nevertheless, when all is said and done, Smith's vision of the self-adjusting, private, market economy remains a profound one. He impressed upon his contemporaries—and in such a forceful, authoritative way that the point could never again be neglected even by critics—the notion that an unregulated economy produces not chaos but coherence and, indeed, many positive social benefits. To have formulated an idea which has been at once a

[3] The term "value" has had different uses among economists, some of which we shall be mentioning as we go along. Unless we specifically state otherwise, however, we shall *always* use the term in a *relative* sense. The *value* of a commodity (service, factor of production, etc.) is then defined as *the quantity of some other commodity (service, factor of production, etc.) for which the given commodity will exchange in the market.* In the particular case where the other commodity is money, *value* becomes the same thing as *price.* However, the other commodity need not be money. It could be bananas or shirts. Indeed, in Adam Smith's case, the other commodity was commonly the services of labor.

[4] This water-diamonds problem is a famous one in the history of economics and we shall be coming to it again (p. 50 and p. 53). It is called the *paradox of value.*

great stimulus to productive thought and an object of profound and continuing criticism is an achievement given to few men.

But Smith's defense of *laissez-faire* was not limited to the concept of the "invisible hand." For he was concerned not only with an economy's equilibrium at a particular moment in time but also with its growth and progress *over* time. It is necessary to say a word about this matter as well.

As far as his over-all view of society's prospects was concerned, Smith tended to be reasonably optimistic. Writing when he did, he could not have anticipated the truly enormous potentialities for economic progress created by the Industrial Revolution which, as we have said, was still mainly to come. Nevertheless, there had been signs of progress in Britain and on the Continent in Smith's day and he saw no reason why this should not continue. Or, rather, why it should not continue for a very long period of time, for Smith believed that *ultimately* economic progress would come to a halt. Society would arrive at a "stationary" state, a state, moreover, which was not particularly attractive. A large population would keep wages low. Competition among businessmen for places to invest their capital would keep profits at a minimum. Only the landowner—possessor of the society's scarce land resources—would be comfortably situated.

Still, all this was a long way off. Smith doubted that any country had ever reached this state, the only possible exception being China; and even in the case of China he felt that better laws and institutions (including more competition!) would have permitted further progress. In the meantime, society could enjoy "the cheerful and the hearty state" characteristic of an advancing society.

But why does society advance in the first place? Why does it not simply remain fixed in whatever position it happens to have achieved at any given moment? The main forces making for growth in the Smithian world are as follows:

1. *Population growth:* Like many thinkers of his day, Smith treated population as an economically determined variable. In the advancing state of society, production is expanding, the demand for labor is brisk, wages are high. This encourages the "marriage and multiplication" of laborers and hence a growing population. The expansion of population is thus stimulated by the growth process and is itself an important element in that process.

2. *Expanding markets and increased division of labor:* This is one of Adam Smith's most famous and important points. The phenomenon of the division of labor—the subdivision of a process of production into its component parts which are then handled by specialized labor or machinery—had been noticed by many writers before Smith. What he did was to analyze the process, to stress its importance, and to show some of the conditions necessary for such division of labor to take place. Perhaps his most important statement on this topic was his conclusion that the

division of labor is "limited by the extent of the market." According to Smith, division of labor makes sense only when one can produce for a fairly large market. Since economic growth generally brings expanding markets, the more growth there is the greater the possibilities for increased division of labor. But increased division of labor makes production more efficient and hence is a factor making for increased output—i.e., economic growth. Smith's analysis here is thus suggestive of a cumulative growth process in which growth leads to bigger markets which lead to more division of labor and further growth.[5]

3. *Capital Accumulation:* The third force making for growth—and this is also much stressed by Smith—is the accumulation of capital. Smith characteristically thinks of *capital* as the stock of goods which is used to support "productive" labor. The production process takes time. Someone must accumulate the food, clothing, and tools for the laborer to use in the period between the beginning and end of the production process. Thus society must regularly set aside part of its annual production to provide a fund for the hiring of "productive" workers who will add to future output.[6]

The combined operation of these growth factors produces in Adam Smith's view a happy and advancing society for some time to come. Moreover, he found in this analysis of growth still additional reasons for supporting the doctrine of *laissez-faire.*

These reasons can be seen most clearly in his discussion of the process of capital accumulation. According to Smith, the accumulation of capital requires someone to forgo spending his income on consumption (or on the employment of "unproductive" workers) and to use that income productively. As can be seen, the whole process is based on thrift. "Parsimony" is the great cause of the "increase in capital." "Frugality" is the friend of society, "prodigality" its enemy.

But who can be counted on to provide these publicly beneficial acts of

[5] This idea of a cumulative growth process involving expanding markets and increased division of labor was taken up in the twentieth century by the American economist Allyn Young in a celebrated article, "Increasing Returns and Economic Progress," *Economic Journal,* Dec., 1928. For a more detailed discussion of Adam Smith's views on this matter, see, in this Series, my *Economic Development—Past and Present,* 2nd ed., Chapter 1.

[6] There is a distinction between "productive" and "unproductive" labor that runs through classical economics. This distinction (seldom used in modern economics) is between labor that produces a tangible product that can be accumulated (wheat, shoes, etc.) and labor which produces services (servants, opera singers, government officials, etc.) In criticism, it has often been said that the distinction between goods and services is basically artificial—opera singers add to the national product just as farmers do. A more sympathetic interpretation is that Smith was pointing up the difference between (a) those acts of production that return a profit to the capitalist and (b) those that do not. Profits, in turn, are considered important because they are a main source of saving and investment in the economy. On the whole, there is no need for the non-specialist to concern himself much about this point. What everyone should remember, however, is that (1) capital accumulation is important and (2) the accumulation process typically does require, as the classical writers stressed, someone to forgo present consumption for future gain.

saving and investment? Not the government. For the state, in Smith's view, tends to be wasteful and extravagant; indeed, all of its officials—officers of justice and war, the whole army and navy, even the sovereign himself!—are essentially "unproductive." However necessary they may be to society for certain limited purposes, they add nothing whatever to its stock of capital. But contrast this with private parties. Competition and self-interest alike drive private individuals to endless exertions on behalf of augmenting their capitals. He puts it this way:

> The uniform, constant, and uninterrupted effort of every man to better his condition, the principle from which public and national, as well as private opulence is originally derived, is frequently powerful enough to maintain the natural progress of things towards improvement, in spite both of the extravagance of government, and the greatest errors of administration. Like the unknown principle of animal life, it frequently restores health and vigour to the constitution, in spite, not only of the disease, but of the absurd prescriptions of the doctor.

This is an extremely strong statement. It argues not only that private actions are the sole source of economic improvement but that they are so vigorous that they can typically sustain that improvement even while supporting an improvident and extravagant government. The state is seen as a burden on society—sometimes required, usually sustainable—but a burden nonetheless, contributing nothing to progress. It is on the "frugality and good conduct of individuals" that all hopes for the future must rest.

And with this additional argument, Adam Smith's case for the "system of natural liberty" is complete.

MALTHUSIAN PESSIMISM

Adam Smith's work established the foundations of classical economics in terms of problems, concepts, and general ideology—but he did not finish the building. As we have said, the *Wealth of Nations* is a great, sprawling work, full of insight and interest, but also digressive, incomplete, and sometimes inconsistent. It needed systematization and development; and, indeed, such a process occurred in the decades following. The result was that classical economics became an integrated body of thought capable of producing at least some answer to almost any economic question put to it.

One rather surprising aspect of this subsequent development was the growing pessimism of classical thought. One might have expected it to be otherwise, for, if Smith wrote on the eve of the Industrial Revolution, these later writers lived in the very heart of it. The growth of a pessimistic outlook at the time of what was possibly mankind's most dramatic economic breakthrough is something of a puzzle, though perhaps it mainly proves the well-known point that the age hardest to understand is one's own. Moreover, in the particular case of the British Industrial Revolution, the *immediate* changes were often far from pleasant. The tremendous wrench in social habits required to transform an agrarian into an industrial society is never an easy one, and in early nineteenth-century England, where the consciences of the well-to-do were not easily disturbed, the coming of machines, factories, and modern industry was often accompanied by rural distress, pauperism, unemployment, child labor, and other assorted ills. It was not at all difficult to take the grim view.

The man and the theory usually held responsible for this increasingly gloomy outlook are Thomas Robert Malthus (1766-1834) and his theory of population. In a sense, this gives Malthus both more and less credit than is his due. It gives him more credit because he was not the sole originator of his population theory—others, even including Smith, had held similar views before him—and because he was not always completely consistent about what that theory was. It gives him less credit because it takes attention from the fact that he concerned himself with many other subjects besides population, including some very interesting speculations about the causes of depressions ("universal gluts") that were taken up again in the '30's of our own century. He can also be given some credit for being the first *professional* economist, since, although it was Reverend Malthus, he was also a professor of political economy in the East India College in Haileybury. It should be added, however, that the character of his work was, in many ways, less "professional" than that of the retired stockbroker, David Ricardo, whom we shall come to in a moment. Malthus had many deep and challenging insights, but system and logic sometimes eluded him.

The theory in question was presented to the world by Malthus in *An Essay on the Principle of Population as it Affects the Future Improvement of Society,* the first edition of which was published in 1798. The immediate cause of his writing the *Essay* was a discussion with his father about the perfectibility of man and society, young Malthus wishing to show that such eighteenth-century optimists as William Godwin and the Marquis de Condorcet were far too hopeful in their philosophies. The effect of the *Essay* was dramatic, both immediately and in the long-run. It went through six editions and had a direct impact on the views of contemporary economists. Later in the nineteenth century, it deeply influenced Charles Darwin in his thinking about the problem of evolution and natural selection. The essayist Thomas Carlyle was so disturbed by his reading of it that he labeled economics the "dismal science," a name which has persisted to this day. In the twentieth century, the *Essay* has been indispensable reading for anyone interested in the problems of the underdeveloped countries. Indeed, in many respects, Malthus' concerns are far more relevant for the economies of India and China today than they proved to be for the British economy of the nineteenth century.

19

The analysis which produced such a stir can be described in a very few words. As Malthus originally presented it, the problem consisted in a contrast between two "ratios":

> Malthus argued that population, unless checked, would tend to double every 25 years, thus growing at a *geometric ratio:* 1, 2, 4, 8, 16, 32, etc. Food production, on the other hand, could at best be expected to grow at an *arithmetic ratio:* 1, 2, 3, 4, 5, 6, etc. Since no matter how well-provided the population was at the outset the operation of these two progressions would soon produce an untenable situation, it was clear that population growth could not continue without some checks.

Where Malthus' pessimism showed through was in his discussion of the possible "checks" to population growth. He divided these into *positive checks,* or those raising the mortality rate, and *preventive checks,* or those reducing the birth-rate. All these checks, in turn, were resolvable into "moral restraint, vice, and misery." According to Malthus:

> "Moral restraint" was "restraint from marriage which is not followed by irregular gratifications." He approved this preventive check but doubted that it would carry enough weight to keep other checks from operating.
> "Vice" included "promiscuous intercourse, unnatural passions, violations of the marriage bed, and improper arts to conceal the consequences of irregular connexions." Needless to say, clergyman Malthus could not countenance such behavior; this left him therefore with no alternative but the third group of checks.
> "Misery" was what was left over—the effect of plague, famine, war, all those positive checks by which either nature or man himself brought the number of human beings under effective control.

In a word, then, Malthus feared that the tremendously potent powers of human population growth would be kept from completely outstripping the food resources of the world largely by the positive check—"misery." Any improvement in the standard of living of the mass of workingmen would immediately lead to an expansion of population and this, in turn, would bring the standard of living back down to a "subsistence" level. As long as its passions and moral character remained unchanged, mankind was chained to the wheel of perpetual poverty.

This picture of dismal economic prospects seems extraordinarily out of place when, with hindsight, we consider what was happening in the emerging European economy of Malthus' day. Furthermore, the picture is conceptually unsatisfying. There is clearly a misplaced precision in the use of the *geometric* and *arithmetic* ratios in the Malthusian account; and although these ratios helped give his essay a dramatic quality and hence a much greater impact than it might have had in more sober dress, they do not do much to recommend it a century and a half hence. Nevertheless, the importance of the Malthusian ideas must not be overlooked, particularly their importance for the evolution of modern economics. For classical economics in the nineteenth century does not wear the relatively cheerful garb in which it had been clad by Adam Smith, but the much more pessimistic garment fashioned by Malthus. And one reason this occurred was that Malthusian thought had a profound effect on the economist who was to give classical economics its most consistent and systematic presentation. This is the third and last great representative of the classical school we shall be able to mention—the remarkable David Ricardo.

THE RICARDIAN SYSTEM

Of all those who attempted to portray the logical implications of the economics of Adam Smith, pride of place undoubtedly should go to the British economist David Ricardo (1782-1823) whose *Principles of Political Economy and Taxation* (1817) was the vehicle by which many of the important classical ideas were carried down to posterity. Ricardo came to economics late; he was a businessman during most of his life, making a fortune on the stock exchange and retiring at age forty-two. But he was the prototype of the modern economist. It has been said that everyone is aware of most of the "truths" of economics; the problem is to build them into a self-contained and consistent structure. Ricardo was such a builder.

As far as his general approach is concerned, Ricardo shared most of the characteristic classical views on fundamentals. Thus, he was a firm believer in the doctrine of *laissez-faire*. Since he was not given to large philosophico-political statements (though he had an interest in public affairs and was once a member of Parliament), one cannot find ringing professions of faith in his work. But the doctrine is unmistakably there, in his policy recommendations and in the clear implications of his analysis.

He also believed that money was largely a veil that could be lifted aside so that the basic laws of production and distribution could be more readily apprehended. For the most part, Ricardo accepted an analysis of money which had been developing since the sixteenth century and which is usually called the *quantity theory of money*. According to this theory, the level of money prices in the economy is proportional to the quantity of money in the economy. But though money affects money prices, it has no direct effect on the *real* variables of the system. Thus, Ricardo, in the classical vein, felt safe in analyzing fundamental economic problems as though they occurred in a money-less world.[7]

Finally, like Adam Smith, he approached the problem of exchange value from the cost of production side. The utility of a commodity—the satisfaction

---

[7] Malthus was more worried about the role of money than Ricardo or Smith and thus, along with the mercantilists, can be cited as anticipating views that were to become important later. See Chapter 6.

it brings to consumers—is "absolutely essential" if the commodity is to have any value at all, but the amount of utility is in no way correlated with that commodity's value. In his illustration of the *paradox of value,* Ricardo substitutes gold for Smith's diamonds but the point he is making is identical.

The fact that Ricardo spent much of his time developing the implications of a given system of thought was a source both of strength and of weakness in his analysis, for classical economics had much merit and also definite limitations. The strength can be illustrated by the contributions Ricardo was able to make in the field of international trade theory. The mercantilists had sometimes argued that the only gain a country could secure in trade was a favorable balance with its accompanying inflow of treasure. Smith had rejected this position, but without great precision or proof. Ricardo took the argument much further and showed how in general mutually beneficial trade could take place between two nations; not one but *both* countries could benefit by concentrating on the production of goods in which they enjoyed relative production advantages. This was an important proposition that remains of interest to economists to this day.[8]

The element of weakness can best be shown in connection with the Ricardian theory of value. Actually, the great problem for both Smith and Ricardo lay in the very first step whereby they dispensed with utility and decided to concentrate on the "cost" side in explaining the values of different commodities. Ricardo tried to look beneath "cost" to the fundamentals that lay behind it and, in the end, he accepted, as an approximation and in modified form, what is usually called the *labor theory of value.* This theory explains the relative values of commodities in terms of the quantities of labor expended on their production. Why does a house cost five times as much as a carriage? Because, so the theory goes, it takes five times as much labor to produce a house as it does to produce a carriage. Ricardo was aware of the weaknesses of this theory but, with the general approach he was using, he could not do much better. The later consequences of his inability to find a better theory were—as we shall see in the next chapter—rather formidable.

Even this example, however, brings out certain of Ricardo's theoretical virtues. The main reason he spent so much time trying to make the labor theory of value work was that he needed a definite theory of value to complete his full theoretical system. He was not content, as Smith had been, to leave the matter hanging. The consequence was that Ricardo produced a general theory of production and distribution which, for its time, was a model of consistency. This theory, while adopting the same general approach Smith had used, nevertheless incorporated the pessimistic views of Malthus with respect to population and food production.

[8] The Ricardian analysis here is usually referred to as the doctrine of *comparative advantage.* This topic is discussed in this Series in Peter Kenen, *International Economics,* 2nd ed., Chapter 2. Incidentally, Ricardo must share the credit for this contribution with his contemporary, the much less well-known British economist Robert Torrens.

The "Ricardian system," in its essence, goes as follows:

1. A society's population will expand whenever the wages of labor are above some relatively low "subsistence" level.
2. Food production, however, will be subject to "diminishing returns" as population grows. As we add more and more labor to the land, the additional produce of the additional labor will be less and less.

These first two propositions incorporate the basic Malthusian ideas (though not, of course, in the form of specific ratios). We have the tendency of population to expand whenever the check of poverty is relieved. We also have the inability of food production to keep pace indefinitely because of diminishing returns in the agricultural sector. To complete the system we now add two further propositions:

3. The Ricardian theory of rent: The rent of a piece of land—the income of the landlord—will be equal to the difference between the produce of a given amount of labor (with its tools) on that land and the produce of the same amount of labor on the least good piece of land in use.

The term "Ricardian theory of rent" is really a misnomer since Ricardo was not the first to develop this theory, others, including Malthus, having reached essentially the same conclusions earlier;[9] this, however, is the term by which the theory has been known ever since and we use it for convenience. The theory, as Ricardo usually stated it, was framed in terms of *different qualities* of land. On the poorest land in use, the landlord will be able to charge very little (or essentially zero) rent since this land still exists in abundance and, if he did charge for its use, capitalists and laborers would simply locate themselves elsewhere. On *better* quality land, however, a definite rent can be charged. Indeed, the amount of rent that can be charged is exactly measured by the difference between the produce of this land and that of the poorest land in use. If the rent were any *less* than this, capitalists and labor would all rush to the better quality land and bid up its price. If the rent were any higher, capitalists and laborers could do better by going to the poorer land; in this case, the price of the better land would have to fall. Rent thus has its source in the differential fertility of various pieces of land, and rents for society as a whole will rise whenever the margin of cultivation is pushed out on to more and more inferior land.[10]

The fourth and final proposition is:

4. Capitalists will be willing to accumulate capital—i.e., give support or "advances" to labor over the period of the production process, as in Smith—only when they get a sufficient rate of return, or profit.

[9] Two other British economists could be mentioned as discoverers of the Ricardian theory of rent: James Anderson and Sir Edward West.

[10] Actually, the same basic theory works even if all land is of the same quality but is limited in over-all quantity. We are, however, giving the characteristic Ricardian version.

The capitalist's job is to provide labor with food and tools during the production period (in agriculture, say, from planting to harvest). He will keep increasing this provision, according to this last proposition, only as long as he can acquire adequate profits for his troubles.

With these four propositions in mind, we can now put together the whole system and, indeed, take an Olympian view of the "natural progress" of society. Population is small. A small population means that we are using only the most fertile lands to produce foods. This, in turn, means that rents are low and there is a great deal of income left over to be shared between the capitalists and laborers in the form of profits and wages. Everybody (everybody, that is, except the landlord) is happy. But now begins an inexorable progress which will end only with arrival at a dismal state:

> Since profits are high, capitalists will begin accumulating more capital, or, what it amounts to, bidding for more laborers to support. This bidding process will raise wages above the subsistence level. When wages are above the subsistence level, population will expand. When population expands, the society is forced to move on to poorer quality land to produce the necessary increase in food supply. This, in turn, means diminishing returns and increased rents.

If we pause for a moment and look at this *second* stage of society, we notice that rents have increased and that the amount of product to be distributed between the laborer and his associated capitalist has decreased. Diminishing returns are squeezing the capitalist and laborer at the margin of production, and, on all the better lands, the landlords are taking up the difference.

We can imagine, however, that at this second stage in the process there is still a good deal of income to be shared by the capitalist and the laborer, and hence we can imagine the process beginning again. The capitalist accumulates, wages go up, population increases—and, lo, we are at the *third* stage. Rents are now even higher than before, diminishing returns are even worse, and the capitalist and laborer are in a still tighter bind. How long does the process go on?

> The process continues until the population is so large, the pressure on land so great, and rents so high that (1) wages are at the subsistence level and (2) profits are so low that no capitalists wish to accumulate more capital. At this point, we have reached the stationary state. Since wages are at the subsistence level, population will not grow. Since profits are very low, there will be no further capital accumulation and hence no further force to raise wages. The system has come to a dead halt. Only if there is some external change—for example, an improvement in agricultural methods—will the movement begin again.

This, fundamentally, is the "Ricardian system." [11] It is a remarkable intellectual construction, bringing together under one head the problems of production, growth, distribution of income, and, indeed, most of the major concerns of economists before and since. It is not a pretty theory. The stationary state, which Adam Smith had seen as a distant prospect, has now been updated to a current and very real possibility. This is a harsh world and the intellectual rigor of the argument has the effect of making the laws of nature seem that much more inescapable. But, as far as the evolution of modern economics is concerned, it represents a major milestone in the development of theorizing about the economic universe. To this day, Ricardo remains an economists' economist.

PERSISTENCE OF LAISSEZ-FAIRE

With the writings of Malthus and Ricardo, the atmosphere of classical economics has decidedly changed. The essential optimism of the late eighteenth century has been challenged and, in its place, there is a picture of society struggling with scant hope of success against deep-rooted natural forces.

In view of this change in atmosphere, one might have expected the general ideology of the classical economics to have changed as well. How are we to account for the persistence of the doctrine of *laissez-faire?* Why did it not go down side by side with the optimistic view?

Of course, the truth of the matter is that the *laissez-faire* ideology was not all-dominating among economists in the nineteenth century (or, for that matter, in the late-eighteenth century either). In the next chapter, we shall indicate that many writers qualified the doctrine, some rejecting it root and branch. The doctrine was always far more popular in England than it was on the Continent, or among early American economists, and, even in England, there were always notable objectors.[12]

---

[11] This is necessarily a somewhat abbreviated version of the system, and, in particular, the observant reader will notice that we have not mentioned the labor theory of value in setting it out. The essential reason that we have been able to skip over the value question is that we have presented the system in a basically one-product ("food" is the product we used) formulation. It is when Ricardo tries to show what happens to the price of food in terms of other commodities that he uses his modified version of the labor theory. In particular, he uses it to argue that the price of food will rise as population increases and it becomes more and more difficult (i.e., uses more and more labor) to get additional food from the land.

[12] Thus, for example, protectionism—as opposed to classical free trade—found supporters in many countries during this period. In America, there was Alexander Hamilton's famous *Report on Manufacturers* (1791) and the work of the prominent protectionist Henry C. Carey (1793-1879). In Germany, Friedrich List's *National System of Political Economy* (1840) made a strong case for the protection of infant industries. Moveover, the early nineteenth century also saw a flowering of socialist thought, in France and also in England, as we shall demonstrate in Chapter 3.

Nevertheless, the fact remains that, in England at least, mainstream economic thought in the nineteenth century continued to be deeply impregnated with *laissez-faire* ideas, and this despite the fundamental pessimism of some of her leading economic theorists. The full explanation of this phenomenon is no doubt complex, but part of it almost certainly has to do with the economic position of Britain at the time. Britain was the first nation to experience the Industrial Revolution, and this revolution arrived there with a tremendous outburst of private initiative and energy and quickly made Britain the leading industrial power in a largely agrarian world. In this situation, governmental regulations and restrictions on the domestic economy, often of ancient origin and conceived with fundamentally different social and economic conditions in view, doubtless were in fact more often obstacles to, than agents of, profound and rapid change. Similarly, in the international sphere, Britain had much to lose and little to gain by governmental prohibitions and interventions in foreign trade. As the most advanced industrial nation, her manufactured products could easily compete with other countries in their own domestic markets, and her rapid industrialization required easy, cheap access to raw materials from abroad. What better policy, then, than to urge (on other countries as well as herself) free trade and competition and "hands off" by the state?

But there is also another part of the explanation which has to do, not with the economic conditions of the age, but with the *theories* themselves. For it is important to realize that there is no necessary connection between an optimistic view of the future, on the one hand, and an advocacy of *laissez-faire,* on the other. It is quite possible to believe that natural forces doom mankind to a grinding struggle for survival and yet still to believe that the best way to manage that struggle is through the private market place rather than by government intervention.

And, in one form or another, this is what many of the later classical economists concluded. Bad as the future might seem, they argued, in effect, that government interference would only make things that much worse. Characteristic forms which state intervention took were the Poor Law and the Corn Laws (duties on imported wheat). But providing for the poor in a Malthusian world simply meant that there would be more poor and greater hunger for all. Placing duties on the import of wheat simply meant that the society would be forced to use its own limited land resources more intensively, thus bringing diminishing returns, lower wages and profits, and a nearer approach to the stationary state. Thus, in addition to the more general arguments for preferring private to public initiatives such as Adam Smith had advanced, it could also be concluded that government action would only intensify those fundamental problems on which the case for pessimism was based.

26 So it was that the doctrine of *laissez-faire,* which had been ushered into economics in an atmosphere of hope and harmony, soon came to have the flavor of discord and despair. The private market economy might still perhaps be the best possible system; but, if it was, it certainly functioned in a highly imperfect world.

SUMMARY

Modern economics becomes a definite reality in the late eighteenth and early nineteenth centuries when the classical economists developed their penetrating analysis of the functionings of a market economy.

The founder of classical economics was Adam Smith, whose *Wealth of Nations* remains one of the most influential documents ever written. Smith, in contrast to the mercantilists, grounded his economic analysis firmly in *real* terms both with respect to the central problems of the field and with respect to the subdued role given money in the analysis of those problems. He is most famous, of course, for his advocacy of the doctrine of *laissez-faire,* or the view that the role of government in the economy should be limited and the main business of society carried on through the activities of private individuals operating on the principle of self-interest.

Smith's justification for this doctrine had two main parts. The first consisted in showing how an unregulated market mechanism could, through competition, achieve socially desirable ends such as providing consumers the goods they wanted at reasonable prices. Although his analysis was incomplete, his insight into the competitive mechanism and his concept of the "invisible hand" were highly important for subsequent analytic developments. The second part of his argument involved the analysis of the natural progress of society. Here he called attention to the important roles of population growth, markets and the division of labor, and capital accumulation. Smith was optimistic about the future, particularly if the State—which he saw as extravagant and "unproductive"—kept its hands off, and society's progress was left to frugal, capital-accumulation-minded private individuals.

In the next few decades, classical economics developed both in technical terms and in terms of a change in outlook, under the leadership of such economists as Thomas Robert Malthus and David Ricardo. Malthus contributed a strongly pessimistic note with his analysis of population growth and food resources. If, as he thought likely, the former tended to grow at a geometric ratio and the latter at an arithmetic ratio, then there would have to be a check on population growth or it would completely outstrip its means of subsistence. Lacking confidence in "moral restraint" and disapproving of "vice," Malthus feared that "misery" might prove to be the key restraining factor.

David Ricardo took the basic approach of Adam Smith—belief in *laissez-faire,* emphasis on *real* factors, and stress on cost above utility in determining value—and combined it with Malthusian views on population

27

and food supplies to produce a remarkably systematic theory of the production and distribution of income over time. According to this theory, the natural progress of society was in the direction of a stationary state in which land rents were high but capitalists earned only very low profits and the mass of workingmen was at the subsistence level.

Despite this new pessimism, the doctrine of *laissez-faire* retained strong roots in British economic thought and, indeed, this later analysis seemed only to provide additional (though not very pleasant) reasons for limiting the role of the state in economic life.

Disharmonies and the

Marxian Critique

With the completion of the main work of the classical writers in the first half of the nineteenth century, economics had emerged as a clear and recognizably important field of knowledge. Of course, it was not true to say, as some of the later classical economists implied, that most of the really important economic questions had now been solved. But many of the significant developments in economic thought to our own day have arisen as improvements or corrections of the lines of analysis delineated by these writers.

Interestingly enough, the classical influence was felt not only in mainstream economics but also among those thinkers who subsequently sought to reject the bulk of the classical doctrine. In the course of the turbulent economic change that marked the western world in the early and mid-nineteenth century, such disagreement was inevitable. The industrialization process—vigorous, disruptive, a challenge to all accepted modes of thought—was now spreading beyond England to the Continent and to the New World. Some economists saw hope in this process, but others were unhappy and perplexed, refusing to accept the new industrialism, or, if they accepted it, rejecting the garment of private capitalism in which it was clothed.

It is to the views of these critical, dissatisfied, sometimes revolutionary thinkers—and particularly to the views of the most influential of all the critics, Karl Marx—that this chapter is addressed.

29

HARMONY AND DISHARMONY

The seeds of a fundamentally different viewpoint were already present in the picture of the economic universe that had been drawn by the classical economists. This picture had, on the one hand, presented a comforting image of harmony between private interest and social welfare—individuals guided by competition and their own self-interest naturally secured the basic objectives of society as a whole. On the other hand, there was the increasing pessimism which the later classical economists had displayed about the race between population and the means of subsistence. Moreover, as we must now notice, the classical image of "harmony" was at no time completely unflawed.

Indeed, from the beginning, the classical economists had recognized the possibility that the interests of certain groups in the society might be different from or even opposed to that of the larger community. Adam Smith, as we have seen, tended to be critical of the business classes. But it was really with Ricardian economics that the problem became explicit and serious. It centered around the question of the distribution of society's income and particularly of the income (rents) going to the landlord class. As far as Ricardo was concerned, the landlord class, which neither worked nor accumulated capital but simply was fortunate enough to hold land, contributed relatively little to economic progress. But it did receive an income. Indeed, this income derived precisely from the scarcity of land which Ricardo viewed as the main limitation on the progress of society. With a few exceptions, Ricardo concluded sweepingly, the "interest of the landlord is always opposed to that of the consumer and manufacturer." This begins to sound not like general harmony but basic conflict! [1]

During the course of the nineteenth century, those economists who continued most directly in the classical tradition handled the problem of disharmony in a variety of ways. In America, a latter day Ricardian, Henry George, published his popular *Progress and Poverty* (1879) which contained a sweeping indictment of landowners and proposed to mop up all rents in a great single tax, which would not only relieve society of the burdens of other taxes but would usher in an age of general prosperity. In England, the great John Stuart Mill (1806-1873) approached the matter in a more compre-

[1] The conflict between the landlords and the other classes in society in the Ricardian world can be seen very specifically in the case of the Corn Laws question. As we indicated in the preceding chapter, one of the great questions of public policy in early nineteenth-century England was whether or not to have duties on imported corn (wheat). The landlords would benefit from such duties because the result would be less importation of foreign wheat, more wheat grown at home, and, consequently, higher rents. But the other classes of society—capitalists and wage earners—would suffer thereby lower wages and profits (as a consequence of diminishing returns and higher rents). This conflict is central to Ricardian theory and the attempt to give it a full-scale analysis was one of the main objectives of Ricardo's theoretical writings.

hensive fashion. In his important mid-century summation of classical economics (*Principles of Political Economy,* 1848), he tried to draw a line of distinction between those laws governing the "Production of Wealth" and those governing the "Distribution of Wealth." While the former "partake of the character of physical truths," the latter are "of human institution solely" and could be made "different, if mankind so chose." The notion that production and distribution are independent processes is a complicated one at best,[2] but at least it did suggest an area where improvements might be made and, along with Mill's belief that society could learn to control its population, indicated a potential escape from the harsh "natural laws" of a Malthusian universe. Mill ended his days supporting a mild form of socialism.

But other writers, less constrained by the classical heritage, more determined to redress the evident grievances which the coming of modern industrialization had brought into existence, took their socialism more seriously. What happened in some cases was that the attitude of optimism and faith in the possibilities of a harmonious society, which, in the case of the eighteenth-century physiocrats and early classical economists, had been associated with the celebration of *laissez-faire,* now became associated with a desire to reform, or even totally reconstruct, the foundations of the economic order. If the nineteenth century classical economists foresaw a "dismal" future, so much the worse for them. For there were also "utopias" close at hand if mankind would only reach out and grasp them!

The writings of these so-called *utopian socialists* were highly uneven and sometimes lacking in any real analytic content. The term covers a widely assorted group of men and views. There was the French nobleman, Comte de Saint-Simon (1760-1825), who criticized the French aristocracy and felt that wealth should be distributed according to ability and industry. There was Charles Fourier (1772-1837), who envisioned the future society as organized in "phalanxes" of a few hundred to one or two thousand people who would form self-contained communities living in large apartment-like buildings or "phalansteries." There was the proletarian, self-taught, anarchistic Proudhon (1809-1865), who at the age of thirty-one answered the title of his book, *What Is Property?,* with the angry phrase, "property is theft!" There was also the famous British cotton magnate, Robert Owen (1771-1858), who having made a fortune in textiles, turned his New Lanark factory into a model in which working hours were reduced, conditions of work improved, and pleasant homes built for the laborers. Not content with this, he set about to establish utopias in practice, such as the community he founded in Indiana—appropriately named New Harmony.

[2] Thus, in a market economy, production and distribution are typically closely related processes. This is because the prices of the factors of production (say, wages of labor) are at the same time: (a) "costs" to producers (and thus influence his choice of *methods of production*) and (b) "incomes" to the factors (and thus determine the *distribution of income*.)

The influence of these various writers on mainstream economics was slight. So also, for the most part, was their influence on practical affairs. Robert Owen undoubtedly had a long-run effect on the development of the British working-class movement but most of his own special projects failed. New Harmony, Indiana—dedicated by Owen on July 4, 1826, with a declaration of "mental independence" from private property, irrational religion and marriage—lasted two years and cost Owen most of his fortune; his Grand National union lasted about the same length of time. Charles Fourier's schemes and hopes were even wilder. He saw mankind as working its way up the slope of history to the stage of harmony (though he would then have to work his way down again) in which nature would prove surprisingly benign and man could enjoy a vigorous sex life for most of his then expected 144 years.

There was, in most of this writing, a note of unrealism and wishful thinking. Often it was an optimism about how well people could cooperate with one another independently of their own self-interest. In some cases there was even a rejection of the fundamental industrialization process: a nostalgic hankering after a simpler communal way of life in which machines, capital, wage-labor, and the other disruptive aspects of an industrial society would cease to do their baleful work.

Because of this underlying lack of realism, the utopian socialists failed to produce many new insights into the economic institutions of their day or to show the path by which those institutions were to be re-made. They are, however, of definite importance in the history of economic thought, for they furnished part of the background for a man who *did* provide such insight and direction and, in so doing, exerted a truly enormous influence on the world to come. And that man, of course, was Karl Marx.

THE MARXIAN CRITIQUE

Marx fashioned a new kind of socialism: it was not "utopian," it was "scientific." It was "scientific" because it was supposedly based on an analysis of the development of capitalistic society which made the coming of socialism not merely a wish-fulfilling reform but an *historical inevitability*. Marx did not ignore the forces of industrialization of his age. He devoted a massive amount of energy and thought to analyzing them, spending far less time (and consequently giving rise to endless later controversies among his followers) in describing the communist society which was the ultimate historic goal.

Marx's attitude toward industrialism was in some ways ambivalent. He stressed both its virtues—its increased productivity, its scientific, technological wonders—and its horrors—mechanization, unemployment, child labor, inequalities of wealth and power. In the deepest sense, he never fully resolved this duality in his thought, though the nature of his *attempted* solution is perfectly clear. The horrors of the industrialization process, according to Marx, are due to the fact that the capitalistic system, once the agent of progress, has outlived its usefulness and become an obstacle to that progress. Once that system is (inevitably) overthrown, the horrors of industrialism will disappear and its virtues—enjoyment of the great fruits of modern technology —will be fully manifested.

His General Approach

Karl Marx (1818-1883) was both a powerful scholar and a passionate revolutionary. Born in Germany of an upper middle-class family, he entered the University of Bonn at age 17 to study law, transferred a year later to the University of Berlin to pursue his growing philosophic interests, and eventually took a doctor of philosophy degree from the University of Jena. The bulk of his intensive scholarly writing was done in the British Museum in London, where he had settled in 1849. His revolutionary zeal found expression in various stints as a journalist (his radical ideas having cost him the possibility of an academic appointment in a German university), his writing of the *Communist Manifesto* (with his close friend and collaborator, Friedrich Engels) for the short-lived Communist League of 1848, and his activities with the International Workingmen's Association or "First International" beginning in 1864. Marx suffered for the espousal of his ideas and his life was often hard, sometimes desperate. Indeed, had it not been for the moral and especially financial support of the more comfortably situated Engels it is difficult to see how he could have both survived and written what he did.

The combination of passionate radicalism and sober scholarship is most clearly demonstrated in his writings. A tract like the *Communist Manifesto,* for example, is filled with ringing denunciations of capitalism (a system of "naked, shameless, direct, brutal exploitation") and summonses to the working classes for action ("Workers of the world, unite!"). On the other hand, in his monumental theoretical work, *Capital,* there are stretches of literally hundreds of pages devoted to the most painstakingly minute examination of the economic mechanisms of capitalist society. Marx was extremely well-read and his writings include not only the presentation of his own ideas but an exhaustive critique of previous authorities and numerous empirical examples (usually drawn from the harsh conditions of working-class life in England) to demonstrate his theses. Marx worked on his masterpiece for decades, but the task was so massive that it was unfinished at his death, only one volume having appeared in his lifetime.[3]

The ultimate aim of *Capital,* as Marx stated in the preface to the first edition, was "to lay bare the economic law of motion of modern society." In

---

[3] Volume I of *Capital* was published in 1867. Volumes II and III were published in 1888 and 1894, respectively, under the editorship of Engels. When Engels died, the task of editing the fourth volume was given to the German socialist, Karl Kautsky, who published it under the heading, *Theories of Surplus Value* (1910).

itself, this statement does not differentiate Marx in any conclusive way from the classical economists, for, as we have seen, these earlier writers were also concerned with economic progress over time. There are, however, two rather fundamental ways in which Marx's conception of the problem differed from that of his British predecessors.

In the *first* place, Marx was seeking to find the "law of motion" not just of economic variables within a given institutional framework but also of that institutional framework itself. Whereas the classical economists had (largely) contented themselves with tracing the path of such items as wages, profits, and rents under a capitalistic system, Marx approached the capitalistic system as itself a variable and, in fact, treated this system as a transitory phase in the long-run evolution of society. What the classical economists had taken for "natural laws," Marx claimed were nothing more than relative laws, valid only for a particular (and ultimately doomed) stage of historical development.

This emphasis on the historical evolution of institutions—social and political as well as economic—is central to Marx's thought.[4] His view, briefly, was that underlying all social change there is a fundamental and continuing development of the productive powers of society. This basic evolution of the technology of production, in turn, determines at each stage along the way the characteristic economic institutions, political arrangements, and even intellectual and cultural values appropriate to that stage. It is in this sense that Marx has a "materialist" or "economic determinist" view of history. Ideas, philosophies, politics are all seen as a superstructure built on this more fundamental technological-economic evolution. "Capitalistic" institutions are likewise regarded as a product of the development of the productive powers of society and, like earlier non-capitalistic institutions, they are impermanent and transitory. For the point is that as the underlying productive powers develop, they gradually create *new* basic conditions for which a *given* set of social and economic institutions is no longer appropriate. These *given* institutions then become *fetters* on the expression of the *new* productive powers. They outlive their usefulness and must be replaced by another set of institutions appropriate to the higher stage of economic development.

The way in which the basic disparity between (1) evolving powers of production and (2) outdated institutions expresses itself in the Marxian world is through "class struggles." And this is the *second* fundamental way in which Marx's approach differs from that of the classical economists. The element of

---

[4] Marx was not alone in his emphasis on the importance of history to economics and his criticism of the classical school for their failure to appreciate the relativity of given economic institutions. In mid-nineteenth century Germany there was developing what is usually called the "German Historical School" whose members (e.g. Wilhelm Roscher, Bruno Hildebrand, Karl Knies, and, somewhat later, Gustav Schmoller and Werner Sombart) criticized the deductive methods of mainstream economics and called for more intensive historical research. In this respect, then, Marx was part of a somewhat larger tradition of German historical economists.

conflict which occasionally mars the harmonies of the classical world becomes, in Marx, the absolutely dominant feature of social life. *All history* is the history of class-struggles. In the case of capitalistic society, the battle has narrowed down to two distinct classes: the capitalists, who control the means of production, and the proletariat, who depend on the capitalists for work. It is not just that the interests of these two groups are sometimes at odds; in the Marxian world, they are characteristically and inevitably opposed. For the dominating aim of the capitalist is to exploit the laborer so that he can increase his profits. *Capital* is filled with examples of such exploitation— lengthening the working-day, speeding up machinery, exploiting the labor of women and children, forcing down wages, and so on. This exploitation derives not from the mean and unsavory character of the capitalist (though Marx would hardly qualify as a friend to the businessman) but from the nature of the capitalist system which requires the capitalist to keep making profits, accumulating capital, making more profits, accumulating further capital, in a continuing spiral, independently of his personal characteristics. The result of this worsening exploitation is that the two classes become completely polarized and conditions become ripe for the overthrow of the capitalists by an increasingly united proletariat. Capitalism, in effect, creates the conditions which make for its own undoing. Or, to put it more accurately, the fact that society's productive powers have outgrown the capitalistic system manifests itself in increasingly sharp class antagonism which spells capitalism's doom.

So spoke Karl Marx.

Value and Capital

Now, however, we must pause and, as in the case of Adam Smith's quite different conceptions, ask the question: But why? What manner of analysis supports the dire Marxian conclusions? And when we turn to Marx's actual analysis we come upon the somewhat surprising discovery that Marx was very much in the tradition of the British classical economists whose teachings he so roundly criticized. The greater portion of the purely analytic content of *Capital* can be construed as a modification and extraordinary elaboration of the value theory of Ricardian economics. Though, of course, elaboration can also make all the difference.

We may set out certain central features of Marx's theoretical structure in a series of propositions about value and capital as he conceived them under capitalistic conditions:

1. Labor is the source of all value.

It is often the case in economics (or, indeed, in any field) that the *first* step is the crucial one and this is very much the case in Marx's analytic structure. We recognize this statement as a version of the "labor theory of value" which we encountered in the theory of Ricardo. It should be noted im- **35** mediately, however, that Ricardo and Marx viewed this theory in somewhat different ways. For while Ricardo used the labor theory only as an approximation and in a very modified way, Marx regarded the theory as a fundamental law. Since it can be shown (as Marx realized) that exchange-values (relative prices) do not uniformly "obey" this law, he was required to say that the "value" of a commodity was something *different* from its exchange-value. For Marx, the "value" of a commodity is given by the labor embodied in it in an absolute sense—i.e., even if commodities do not actually exchange or tend to exchange at their true "values." [5]

> 2. Labor is paid in wages its own value, this being essentially the amount of labor required to rear, train, and maintain the life of the laborer.

This second proposition can be interpreted as an application of the labor theory to the purchase of labor. It takes a certain amount of labor to feed, clothe, educate, and perpetuate a member of the labor force; this amount will determine his value and his wages.

> 3. The capitalist employs laborers for more hours than is necessary to maintain the laborers and hence is able to secure a surplus-value which comes to him in the form of profit. [6]

Suppose it takes a laborer on the average 6 hours a day to produce the quantities of commodities necessary to maintain himself. The capitalist will employ the laborer not for 6 hours but for 12 hours say. This means that the additional 6 hours produce a surplus above the wages paid to labor which the capitalist may dispose of as he sees fit. This extraction of surplus-value from labor is what Marx means by exploitation.

> 4. The most important and typically dominating aim of the capitalist is to increase this surplus value.

Here we have a comment on the sociology of capitalistic production. The capitalist, in the Marxian world, is not interested in producing large quantities of useful commodities for their own sake, nor is he even much interested in consuming luxury goods himself, though occasionally he will give himself up to such pastimes. The main driving urge of the capitalist is to

[5] Even Ricardo had an occasional tendency to look at "value" in this absolute sense, though he was more vague about the matter and did not make it the core of his theory. Whether the Marxian notion of absolute value has more than a definitional significance (i.e., What is the "value" of commodity *A? Def*. It is the labor embodied in the production of commodity *A*) is a matter on which Marxists and non-Marxists are likely to differ. For an interpretation sympathetic to Marx's position, see Paul M. Sweezy, *The Theory of Capitalist Development* (New York: Oxford University Press, 1942), especially Part One.

[6] In a more detailed examination of Marxist thought, we should have to recognize that the "profits" of an individual capitalist are not exactly the same as his "surplus-value" and also that "profits" can be subdivided into interest, rents, etc. However, our concern here is only with the fundamentals of the system.

force a continuing expansion of surplus values. This is the life-blood of the entire system.

> 5. The capitalist attempts to augment his surplus value by accumulating capital in its two basic forms: variable capital (the labor he hires) and constant capital (raw materials, tools, machinery).

Marx divides the factors of production into two fundamentally different categories. One—variable capital—involves the direct purchase of labor power by the capitalist. The other—constant capital—involves the purchase of commodities (machinery, etc.) which are the products of past labor, or labor in the hands of other capitalists. The significance of this distinction becomes clear in the following:

> 6. The employment of constant capital (machinery, etc.): (a) greatly increases total production; (b) causes technological unemployment—the industrial reserve army of the unemployed—and hence keeps wages down; but (c) does *not* create surplus-value, this achievement being restricted to variable capital (labor).

With this sixth proposition, we come near to the heart of what Marx believed were the internal "contradictions" of the capitalistic system. For while Marx recognized the great potential inherent in the use of machinery, he also claimed that, under capitalism, the introduction of machinery would not represent a clear-cut benefit either to the laborer or the capitalist. In the case of the laborer, indeed, the reverse is true. For, in the Marxian world, the introduction of machinery invariably displaces labor and thus creates a condition of *relative* over-population. Marx rejected the Malthusian notion that population pressure in the biological sense would keep wages down. But essentially the same result can be achieved if by introducing machinery the capitalist can create an industrial reserve army of the unemployed and thus establish a surplus of population *relative* to jobs. For with unemployment rampant, wages are certain to be kept down at or very near the subsistence level.

As for the capitalist himself, the problem with the introduction of machinery is that, ultimately, it is displacing the real source of his surplus value—i.e., labor. For in calling machinery *constant* capital, Marx means precisely that it does not undergo any increase in value as it is translated from the input to output. The capitalist who takes labor to *produce* a machine is able to extract surplus value from that labor and to include it in the price of the machine. But the capitalist who then buys and *uses* the machine has already paid for the full value of the machine and can extract no further surplus from it. This follows from the premise that labor and only labor is the source of all value. Hence the use of machinery is a two-edged sword for the capitalist: by causing unemployment it keeps wages down and thus permits a continuing exploitation of labor, but, at the same time, this machinery fails in what is the ultimate purpose of capitalist production—the creation of surplus value.

Marx's primary objective, we recall, was to unveil the "economic law of motion" of capitalistic society. How are the foregoing propositions related to the forces making for change in the Marxian world? More particularly, how do they operate to produce the inevitable downfall of capitalism?

The answers to this question are not easily found in Marx, partly because he did not live to put his work in final form, and partly (one suspects) because his underlying theoretical structure is not strong enough to bear the weighty conclusions he wished to place upon it. Certain *elements* of an answer can, however, be clearly discerned.

In the *first* place, Marx argues that there is a long-run tendency under capitalism for the employment of constant capital (machines) to increase relative to variable capital (labor). Or, as Marx puts it, there is a continuing increase in the *organic composition* of capital.[7] The causes of this increase lie in the capitalists' passion for accumulation combined with their need to keep wages low. If capitalists were to direct themselves to the accumulation of variable capital (labor), wages would be certain to rise. To prevent this, they introduce more and more machinery, thus replenishing the industrial reserve army and keeping wages down. The consequences of this process are, for the workers, "immiseration" and, for the capitalists, a "falling rate of profit." The falling rate of profit is deduced from the assumption that surplus-value is extracted from variable capital only and that the proportion of variable capital to total capital is declining.[8] Although Marx qualified this law of a falling rate of profit, he clearly considered its "proof" a feather in his cap. "Since this law is of great importance for capitalist production," he wrote, "it may be said to be that mystery whose solution has been the goal of the entire political economy since Adam Smith."

But there are further problems in capitalistic development besides the continuing misery of the masses and the falling rate of profits. There is, in the

---

[7] If v is variable capital and c is constant capital and if o is the organic composition of capital, then, by definition,

$$o = \frac{c}{c + v}.$$

[8] In this part of his analysis, Marx assumes that the amount of surplus value (s) extracted from each unit of variable capital (v) remains constant—i.e., that:

$$\frac{s}{v} = k$$

The rate of profit (p) is defined as: $p = \dfrac{s}{c + v}$.

On the assumption that $\dfrac{s}{v} = k$, it can be shown by elementary algebra that a rising organic composition of capital $\left(\dfrac{c}{c + v} \right)$ implies a falling p. Of course, the problems in this analysis are not with the algebra but with the validity of the assumptions and hypotheses on which the analysis is based.

second place, a tendency for capital to become concentrated in larger-scale productive units and for control over production to become centralized in the hands of the few. According to Marx, the constant accumulation of means of production by the capital naturally leads to large-scale production, and this is abetted by the superior competitive ability of large over small firms and by capitalistic institutions such as the banking and credit system. One result of this tendency is that, as small capitalists are driven out of business and fall into the ranks of the proletariat, the polarization of the two classes— capitalists and laborers—becomes increasingly sharp. Another result is that capitalistic production, though still formally *private* in its property relations, becomes more and more *social* in its intrinsic character. Large-scale production transforms the individual workman into part of a vast social productive process and the capitalist owner of the means of production into a trustee of society. Thus, paradoxically, according to Marx, if we look at underlying trends, we find that "the capitalist mode of production abolishes private property and private labor."

In the *third* place, finally, Marx argued that capitalistic production develops in a rhythm of expansion and contraction that is punctuated by crises that become increasingly severe. That Marx had a definite perception of what modern economists call the "business cycle" is beyond doubt. What is less clear is his theory of the causes of this cycle and their relationship to the fundamental nature of capitalistic production. In terms of the propositions we discussed in the last section, it would seem that Marx saw a fundamental conflict between the *effect* of capitalistic production and its *aim*. The *effect* of capitalistic mechanization of production is a great increase in society's productive powers (proposition 6a.); the *aim,* however, has little to do with increased production, but rather with the accumulation of capital and surplus value (proposition 4). The implication is that the organization of society under capitalism is inadequate to absorb the vast increases of productivity that this organization generates, and that crises inevitably result.[9]

However sketchy the details, the cumulative impact of these various "laws of motion" is all too easy to discern. Mechanization, immiserization, falling profit rates, crises, concentration of capital—all these forces work toward intensifying the class struggle which is the mechanism of fundamental change. The laborer—exploited, poverty-ridden, threatened with unemploy-

[9] In Volume III of *Capital* (published in unfinished form after Marx's death), there appears the following capsule description of the cause of crises which the reader can attempt to evaluate for himself: "The stupendous productive power developing under the capitalistic mode of production relatively to population, and the increase, though not in the same proportion, of capital values (not their material substance), which grow much more rapidly than the population, contradict the basis, which, compared to the expanding wealth, is ever narrowing and for which this immense productive power works, and the conditions under which capital augments its value. This is the cause of crises." For a summary of various possible interpretations of Marx on crises, see again, Sweezy, *op. cit.,* especially Part Three.

ment—is united by the very social process of capitalistic production into a force capable of revolutionary action. The capitalist, under the sword of falling profits and recurrent crises, is forced to step up this exploitation of the laborer, thus adding further fuel to the fires of discontent. They stand now in naked opposition—capitalists and proletariat, defenders of the dying order and the creators of the new.

Inevitably, with the sanction and ordination of history, the revolution does finally come. The expropriators are expropriated and a new society is born. What manner of new society? Again the full details are lacking, but the central thrust is clear. It will be a society in which the full forces of modern productive technology can be expressed relieved of the contradicting constraints of the capitalistic order. And it will be a society in which, classes having disappeared, the class struggle which has dominated all previous history will, at last, come to an end.

MARXISM
AS THEORY AND IDEOLOGY

What are we to make of all this? Is it sense, nonsense, a portion of each? How can one deal with such highly inflammatory materials?

There is perhaps no fully satisfactory way of evaluating such a controversial figure as Marx, but at least a start can be made if we separate Marxist thought as economic analysis in a somewhat narrow sense from Marxist thought as a more general ideology of revolutionary change. For, although he has strengths and weaknesses in both departments, they are not characteristically the same strengths and weaknesses.

Marx's Economic Theory

As far as economic analysis is concerned, it might seem that Marx's contribution was rather slight. His work was premised on a theory of value which was already antiquated even at the time he wrote, and many of his deductions from this premise are, to say the least, questionable. As we shall see in the next chapter, mainstream economics in the last decades of the nineteenth century paid little attention to Marx's formulation of the problems to be solved and rejected the tools he used to solve them. Some of the greatest theorists of this next period—such as Alfred Marshall and Léon Walras—barely acknowledge Marx's existence. And, to some degree, this has been true of the mainstream of Western economic thought ever since.

Such an evaluation, however, overlooks a more subtle interpenetration of Marxian ideas into our ways of thinking about economic problems. Unlike classical economics, Marx's theory is a headlong assault on the problems of industrialization in its modern form. He conceived the problem on a grand scale and, in so doing, developed many insights which have colored subsequent approaches to modern industrialization and, in some cases, have cropped up again in the form of later, more or less independent, discoveries.

Perhaps the most important of these insights was his awareness of the historical relativity of given social institutions and the importance of the economic element in the process of historic change. He was almost certainly wrong in associating capitalistic institutions with a particular phase of the industrialization process [10] and he undoubtedly overstressed the economic-technological element as the sole determinant of change. Nevertheless, he did understand clearly that the institutions of any particular age are not given by "nature" but are evolving, historically influenced structures and that the forces of technology and production affect many areas of man's life beyond the confines of narrow economic relationships. No reflective person in the modern world would care to deny either point.

Moreover, Marx pointed up many aspects of industrial life which had either escaped attention or were underemphasized in classical economics. One such was his awareness of the importance of mechanized, large-scale production as not the exceptional but the *typical* form of advanced capitalistic enterprise. Another was his awareness of the problem of the cycle of expansion and contraction of industrial production, this cycle being viewed not as an occasional aberration due to speculation or momentary crises of confidence, but as an intrinsic part of the growth process. Marx was not alone in these discoveries and his analysis of them, as we have seen, was far from complete; nevertheless, he did foreshadow a number of later developments which were to occupy economists to our own day.

Thus, any comment about the deficiencies of Marx's analysis should be qualified by a recognition of the important advances he made. At the same time, *neither* should one be blind to those deficiencies which are real and, in some cases, glaring. His attempt to deal with the problem of relative prices in terms of *two* theories—a theory of "value" and a theory of "prices of production" [11]—has been rightly regarded by most Western economists not

[10] He was really wrong at, so to speak, "both ends." That is to say, capitalistic institutions have shown a degree of durability even in the most advanced industrial societies which far outdistanced Marx's anticipations. Mature industrialization has not brought the breakdown of capitalistic institutions he predicted. But he was also proved wrong at the other "end"—that is, about the *early* stages of industrialization. For he assumed (with some qualifications) that capitalism was the historically necessary form of the first stages of industrialization and yet this has not proved universally the case. There is a definite irony in this, because it has been communist revolution which has upset his predictions. Modern China—a country clearly in the early stages of industrialization—should, by Marxist logic, be capitalistic, but, in fact—in the name of Marx—it has turned to communism.

[11] The reason Marx had to develop two theories was that he recognized (rightly) that under competitive conditions the rate of profit would have to be the same in different industries (otherwise, producers would shift from low to high profit industries). But he knew that the organic composition of capital was very different in different industries. If products sold at their "values," industries using a great deal of variable capital (labor, the only source of surplus value) would make a higher rate of profit than those using relatively greater quantities of constant capital (machines). His solution,

only as a failure but as an unfruitful failure—i.e. a failure that has led to no particularly interesting amendments or corrections.

Equally, perhaps more, important was his failure to incorporate in his systematic theory the full effects of technological change. This may seem surprising since Marx was aware of the powers of modern technological advance and stressed them on a number of occasions. In the actual analysis, however, the matter becomes very muddy indeed. Thus, Marx's demonstration of a "falling rate of profit" is compatible with significant technological progress, in his own examples, only on the assumption that the wages of employed labor (in commodity terms) are rising. But Marx also wishes to insist on the "immiserization" of labor. If he allows for full technological progress and continues to insist on "immiserization," then he has failed to demonstrate a falling profit rate. If, on the other hand, he wishes to retain both falling profits and immiserization, then his examples must be interpreted as a denial of the importance of technological progress.[12] This is not merely a technical detail. For the weakness of the analysis here helps account for an overwhelmingly important defect in Marxian predictions about the progress of capitalism—namely, his failure to foresee the enormous improvements in the standard of living of the laboring classes that modern industrialization under essentially capitalistic conditions was to bring about. This failure may easily reflect the essential duality in Marx's thought between the horrors and the wonders of industrialism which we have mentioned earlier. Whatever its source, however, the fact is that the historical disproof of the growing immiserization of the working people under capitalism is enough to reduce Marx's general theory of increasing class conflict and the breakdown of capitalism to ashes. As far as useful predictive analysis is concerned, it relegates Marxism to the category of historical relics.

Marxism as an Ideology

But Marxism, considered in a broader sense, is clearly *not* an historical relic. It is a dynamic, infectious ideology of the present-day twentieth-century world commanding the professed allegiance of literally hundreds of millions of people. How—in view of the obvious imperfections of the analysis—could this possibly be?

---

in essence, was to average out the total surplus value of all capitalists over all industries and to say that "prices of production" (as opposed to "values") are those which guarantee equal profit rates to all. This procedure seems to have little merit beyond making an unworkable theory appear to "work."

[12] As we indicated in an earlier note (p. 38), Marx's demonstration of a falling rate of profit includes the assumption of a constant rate of exploitation (i.e., $s/v = k$). If, owing to technological progress, a given quantity of labor is producing *more* commodities, then a given rate of exploitation implies an increase *in commodity terms* of both wages per worker and surplus value per worker. But if this is the case, then "immiserization" (at least in the sense of low or falling wages per employed worker) must go by the board.

The simpler part of the answer can be given by the statement that present-day Marxism is by no means an exact equivalent of what Marx taught in the middle of the nineteenth century. Toward the end of his life, Marx himself commented half-ironically: "I am not a Marxist." And it is clear that in the century since the first volume of *Capital* appeared, there has been a constant process of interpretation, re-interpretation, amplification, modification, and in some cases, a virtual re-writing of Marx's doctrines. There have been the "orthodox" Marxists and the "revisionists." There was Lenin, who, in the period leading up to the Russian Revolution, developed Marxian theory as an explanation of "imperialism" and, with little regard for historical trends and inevitabilities, forged the strategy of overthrow in a society that had barely entered upon its "capitalistic" phase. There was Stalin who in the late 1920's and 1930's used communism to *create* (not to reap the benefits of an already created) modern industrial society, often at cruel expense to the masses of workers and especially peasants. In the 1960's, there has been the ideological split between the Russian Communists (Khrushchev, Kosygin, Brezhnev) and the Chinese (Chairman Mao Tse-tung), each claiming to be the proper heir to Marx and Engels. A few imperfections of analysis clearly need be no bar to the success of a doctrine capable of so many different interpretations as this.

Still, it is *Marx* that these people are interpreting (not, say, Adam Smith or John Stuart Mill) and there remains the question of his special and still-continuing ideological appeal. Although history will have to give the final answer to this question, it is already possible to narrow the matter down. For one of the striking things about Marxist ideology, as many commentators have observed, is that its appeal is greatest *not* in the most economically advanced societies (such as the United States, England, most of Europe) but in relatively underdeveloped countries at the moment of transition to modern industrialization. This fact may pose something of a puzzle for Marxian philosophy, but it also gives some insight into the particular nature of its appeal. For Marx's characteristic view of industrialization—stressing its great potential benefits but also its immediate disruptive, almost inhuman dislocations—gives a fairly precise picture of what the coming of modern industrialism actually *does* to an undeveloped economy. More than that, it provides a theory whereby these dislocations can be blamed on an alien class—either the domestic capitalists or, more characteristically in the very poor countries of today, the foreign, colonial, capitalist exploiters. At the moment of transition, Marxism seems not only "realistic," but emotionally gratifying.

Thus it is that what must be viewed as a weakness in Marxian analysis becomes one of the sources of strength of Marxian ideology. In an economically advanced country where the full fruits of industrialization have been enjoyed by *all* classes of society, the theory seems not only imperfect but irrelevant. In an undeveloped economy, however, both the yearning for economic progress and the desire to charge the price of progress to the account of the "exploiters" are combined in a comfortable Marxist union. That the **43**

appeal of communism is most keenly felt in a temporary stage of development
—i.e., before the benefits of progress have become apparent and widely shared
—is not, however, too much of a comfort for the Western observer. For
experience has also shown that, once in power, communist regimes are quite
capable of sustaining themselves far beyond that transitional stage which was
responsible for their accession. In a sense, this is also a violation of the spirit
of Marx. For it suggests that political structures are not simply the reflection
of a particular phase of economic development. They also—sometimes unfortunately—have a life of their own.[13]

SUMMARY

The classical view of the harmonies of private capitalism was
somewhat marred by a growing pessimism about population and by an awareness of the possibilities of conflicting interests among the various classes of
society. During the early- and mid-nineteenth century, a number of thinkers
tried to find ways of escaping these problems. John Stuart Mill preserved the
classical tradition but espoused a form of socialism. The *utopian socialists*
went further and described ideal societies based on a rather optimistic view
of human nature and without a firm analysis of existing society.

The most important critic of classical political economy, however, was
Karl Marx. Marx diverged sharply from the classical school by interpreting
capitalism as a transitory phase of historical development which had been
created and would be doomed by an underlying process of economic-technological evolution, and also by centering his analysis of capitalism exclusively
on the "class-struggle." Far from seeing harmonies in capitalism, he saw it as
the battle ground between two distinct classes—capitalists and the proletariat
—the ultimate consequence being the overthrow of capitalism and the
emergence of a communist society.

In Marxian analysis, the capitalist is seen as extracting a surplus value
from labor which is the source of all value. In order to prevent wages from
rising, however, the capitalist is forced to substitute machinery (constant
capital) for labor. This causes unemployment and distress in the laboring
class and reduces their wage demands, but (in a typical capitalist contradic-
tion) it also harms the capitalist because machinery is not a source of surplus
value. Thus, capitalism is capable of producing a fall in the profit rate and
immiserization for the working classes at the same time. These developments,
along with the growing concentration of capital and the problem of capitalist
crises, account for the eventual collapse of the capitalistic system.

[13] For an interesting discussion of the range of issues taken up in this last section,
see Adam B. Ulam, *The Unfinished Revolution* (New York: Random House, 1960). For
a discussion of the application of Marxism in communist practice, see, in this Series,
Gregory Grossman, *Economic Systems*.

Marx's detailed analysis owes much to classical and especially Ricardian economics. Its strengths lie in Marx's appreciation of the importance of the process of historical change and his awareness of many features of industrial society such as large-scale industry and the business cycle. Its weaknesses derive from the inadequate labor theory of value on which his concepts of exploitation and surplus value are based, and, even more significantly, from his failure to take full account of the effects of technological change and the benefits it might bring to the working classes.

If the Marxian doctrine has weaknesses as a theory, it has, however, retained a strong ideological appeal, particularly in countries undergoing the transitional process from underdevelopment to modern industrialization. For in these countries, his view of industrialization in terms of potential benefits and immediate dislocations not only seems realistic and appropriate but also provides a convenient whipping-boy—the "capitalist" or "colonial exploiter" —to whom the birth pangs of modern growth can be attributed.

Analytic Progress

in the Late-Nineteenth Century

As we have said, mainstream economics did not take the path indicated by Marx. Although we can find sources for both Marxian and mainstream analysis in classical economics, the divergence between the offshoots becomes greater and greater until, by the end of the nineteenth century, there is virtually no point of contact left.

In this chapter, we return to the mainstream to discuss the progress of theoretical economics during the last few decades of the nineteenth century. There is considerable difference of opinion about the achievements of this period. To some commentators— Marxists, of course, but also many non-Marxists—much of the work of the late-nineteenth century seems sterile, technical, and unrealistic. By contrast, many eminent commentators argue that it was in these decades that scientific modern economics came of age.[1] Even *during* the period there was basic disagreement about what was being achieved. Cambridge University's Alfred Marshall, the

---

[1] For two contrasting recent evaluations of the achievements of late-nineteenth century economics, see O. H. Taylor, *A History of Economic Analysis* (New York: McGraw-Hill, 1960), who takes a rather critical view, and J. A. Schumpeter, *History of Economic Analysis* (New York: Oxford University Press, 1954), who is far more favorable. One of the reasons—not the only one—for this difference of opinion is that Taylor's book is focused mainly on the philosophy and ideology of economics whereas Schumpeter's is much more concerned with economic *analysis* in the narrower sense. As will become clear shortly, late-nineteenth century economics is far more interesting from the latter than from the former point of view.

most famous economist of the age, stressed continuities with the past. But Marshall's British contemporary, William Stanley Jevons, and the great French-Swiss economist, Léon Walras, spoke of "revolutionary" feats and compared their work in economics with that of such giants in the natural sciences as Newton, Laplace and Lagrange.

Why these different evaluations? What exactly *was* happening to analytic economics at this time and what were its roots in the past?

SOME IMPORTANT
GENERAL CHARACTERISTICS

One thing that was not particularly revolutionary about mainstream economics in the late-nineteenth century was its ideology. Not that classical *laissez-faire* ideas were always accepted uncritically. Of the three economists we have just mentioned, Jevons thought each case of government action should be judged on its own merits, Walras was a quasi-socialist, and even the great Marshall was distantly sympathetic to socialist ideals. However, Marshall also felt that there was a danger that "collective ownership of the means of production would deaden the energies of mankind, and arrest economic progress" and, for the time being, he was eager to preserve and protect the "springs of free enterprise." Thus, the prevailing ideology was not radically different from that which had obtained in the classical period. One difference that might be noted, however, was that of tone. The late-nineteenth century saw an increasing *professionalization* of economics. This tended to mean a greater separation between ideology, on the one hand, and analysis on the other. Writers in this period could differ substantially about politics and still find much common ground in their professional work as economists.[2]

In terms of general outlook, there was also an increasing optimism about the future progress of society. Actual economic conditions in the late-nineteenth century in both Europe and America were vastly different from what they had been when the classical writers, and later Marx, had lived. Rapid economic and technological progress in the industrializing societies was now established fact. The English workingman may have suffered abuses

---

[2] This *professionalization* of economics in the late-nineteenth century is a most important feature of the era. At the beginning of the century, as we have said, Malthus was the first professor of economics, but by the end of the century, every country had its full complement of professional academic economists. Economic journals and associations of economists were also being established. In America, the American Economic Association was founded in 1885 and its first president, Francis A. Walker of MIT, came into office in 1886. In that same year, down the river at Harvard University, the *Quarterly Journal of Economics* was founded, and is, of course, very much a flourishing journal to this day. It was becoming increasingly the case that the purpose of economics was not polemical but to "pursue and master purely scientific truths." Even to this day, however, economists will argue as to how far this professionalization of the field should go.

when the factories were first introduced but, by the late-nineteenth century, his real income was clearly and unequivocally rising—and the same was true in America and in many other economically advancing nations. Given this dynamic, progressive state of affairs, the pessimistic outlook of the Ricardo-Malthus variety necessarily gave way to a more sanguine view of the future. Optimism and *laissez-faire* could once again join hands. But the optimism was not based on a new and penetrating theory of the causes of economic progress. On the contrary, such progress tended to be taken for granted and, as far as formal economic analysis is concerned, the problem of how and why growth occurs virtually disappeared from view.[3]

Indeed, taken as a whole, the analytic apparatus developed by economists in the late-nineteenth century represented a certain narrowing of focus. By far the greatest attention was given to a single area of thought—price theory, or, if we wish, the full working out of the mechanism behind Adam Smith's "invisible hand." In attacking this problem, the theorists of this period largely shared two and largely rejected one of the fundamental assumptions of the classical economists.

What they shared was *first* the habit of treating economic situations as though most or all industries were composed of very small firms none of which was large enough to have any effect on the market prices of goods and services. This assumption of *pure competition* was to be challenged explicitly in the next period as the realities of large-scale modern industry came to be taken into account, but for the moment it still ruled the theoretical roost. *Second,* they shared with the classical economists their view of money in relationship to the underlying real economy. That is, they argued that changes in the quantity of money in the economy would mainly affect the over-all price level and would either have no effect, or very little effect, or only a temporary effect, on the real relationships of production and distribution that were their primary interest. These real relationships they analyzed—as had Smith, Ricardo and Mill—as though they virtually occurred in a barter economy.

The element they *rejected*—and this made all the difference—was the view that the problem of exchange-value should be approached exclusively or even primarily from a labor or "cost" standpoint. For the new economics the key word was *utility*. These economists saw *utility* not simply as necessary for value but as influencing value quantitatively and, indeed, providing a concept

[3] The narrowness of late-nineteenth century economists, suggested here, is mainly a characteristic of the formal analysis of the period, not of their more general writings and commentaries. Knowledge was expanding greatly but the demand for greater precision brought certain limits to what could be handled theoretically. Also, it should be pointed out that there were important schools of thought—as, for example, the German historical school, noted in the preceding chapter—who took a quite different approach from the theorists we shall be discussing here. Like Marx, these historical writers were concerned not only with growth but also with the evolution and development of capitalistic institutions. When all is said and done, however, it must be concluded that the *main* drift of the period was towards precision rather than scale with the result that many earlier avenues of thought simply lay fallow.

through which the whole of the micro-economic universe could be comprehended.

That a change in approach in one apparently limited aspect of economic analysis should lead to claims of a "revolution" comparable to that of the Newtonian synthesis in physics may seem rather extravagant. But it is not necessarily so. We have already seen, in the Marxian analysis, how simple premises can be developed into the most elaborate and imposing structures of thought. And, on a certain scale, this was what was happening in mainstream economics in the late-nineteenth century. The economists of the time were not only using utility to help explain why bananas cost more than apples but were also perceiving that the question of why bananas cost more than apples ultimately involves *all other variables* in the economic system. This perception brought forth—not for the first time, but more explicitly than ever before—a new problem and a new method. The problem was that of *general equilibrium;* the method was that of *mathematics.*

Let us trace the process by which this change occurred.

THE MARGINAL UTILITY THEORY

The history of utility analysis in economics suggests some philosophic reflections about the progress of human knowledge. When the time is ripe for a new idea, people everywhere seem to be discovering it or on the verge of discovering it. Before the time is ripe, the very same idea may languish ignored and unheralded. For ideas stand not in isolation but in relation to larger systems of thought, and it is only as these systems mature that new ideas can be effectively used. At this point, indeed, the new ideas seem almost "obvious."

At least something like this seems to have happened in the case of utility analysis. Despite the difficulties of the *paradox of value* (diamonds, gold = expensive; water, air = cheap), the notion that the utility of a commodity was directly related to its exchange value had never altogether departed the corridors of economic thought. While Smith and Ricardo were wrestling with labor and cost, many thinkers—especially such French writers as the Abbé Condillac (1714-1780) and Jean Baptiste Say (1767-1832)—were giving utility pride of place as a determinant of market prices. Unfortunately, a truly systematic application of the concept was out of the reach of these writers; moreover, the concept itself was imperfectly formulated.[4]

[4] This is shown by the difficulties these writers still had with the *paradox of value.* Condillac, for example tried to get around the air-water aspect of the problem by suggesting that we really *do* pay for these useful products because we have to take the trouble of breathing the one and fetching the other. J. B. Say's solution was not much better: air and water, he said, are *so* useful that their value is infinite and therefore we cannot buy them.

In the course of the late-eighteenth and early-nineteenth centuries, however, great progress was made in resolving these difficulties. A number of economists clarified the concept of utility and suggested how it might be applied in economic analysis.[5] By the middle of the nineteenth century, the tools were at hand for an explicit statement of the "new" theory and, indeed, it received such a statement in the hands of the German economist, Hermann Heinrich Gossen (1810-1858), who presented it to the world in 1854 with the claim—similar to some we have already noticed—that he was doing for economics what Copernicus had done for astronomy!

But the world was not yet quite ready for Copernicus—at least not the world of economics. The classical system was still a power to be reckoned with. In 1848—just six years before Gossen's publication—John Stuart Mill had published an improved but still patched-together version of the classical approach to value. "Happily," Mill wrote (unhappily, as it turned out), "there is nothing in the laws of value which remain for this or any future writer to clear up; the theory of the subject is complete." [6] Gossen's personal experience certainly did not prove otherwise. Gossen's idea had no impact; no one bought his book; in the end, he called in the outstanding copies, destroyed them, and died bitter and neglected, unaware that he was soon to be rediscovered and given his proper place in the economics hall of fame.

By 1870, however, the situation was at last "ripe." And then everyone rushed in. In Austria, Carl Menger (1840-1921), in Switzerland, Léon Walras (1834-1910), and in England, Jevons (1835-1882) and Marshall (1842-1924)—each working independently of the others—brought forth the good news. And, thus, what was called the *marginal utility theory of value* was officially and triumphantly launched.

What exactly was the new theory? And why did it cause such a stir?

As far as the substance of the theory is concerned, its essentials can be

[5] A list of writers who either had or almost had the new theory before the middle of the nineteenth century would be very long. Suffice it to mention just a few names: Jeremy Bentham (1748-1832), who was also the founder of the philosophy known as "utilitarianism"; Nassau William Senior (1790-1864), the first professor of political economy at Oxford; Auguste Walras (1801-1866), father of the eminent Léon; Jules Dupuit (1804-1866), a distinguished professional engineer; not to mention the earlier forerunner, Daniel Bernouilli (1700-1782), who resolved the so-called St. Petersburg Paradox with the aid of utility theory; and several others. (For a statement of the St. Petersburg Paradox and Bernouilli's approach to it, see, in this Series, R. Dorfman, *The Price System,* pp. 72-74.)

[6] This quotation gives a somewhat misleading impression of Mill's contributions to value theory (which were several) and his general contributions to economics (which were numerous). Space does not permit a real treatment of Mill's work, but the reader can find a succinct statement of his contributions in the essay "The Nature and Role of Originality in Scientific Progress" in George J. Stigler, *Essays in the History of Economics* (Chicago: University of Chicago Press, 1964). Stigler's book also contains a highly useful summary of the development of the utility theory we are discussing, in his essay, "The Development of Utility Theory."

stated in a definition and two propositions about human psychology. The definition is that of *marginal utility* which can be given roughly as follows:

> The *marginal utility* of a commodity is the addition to our total utility (satisfaction) occasioned by the last unit of the commodity in our possession.

The focus on *marginal* as opposed to *total* utility is absolutely central to the theory. Whether the commodity be meat or potatoes or, for that matter, water or diamonds, we are concerned with the *addition* to total utility occasioned by our having an extra unit of the commodity in question. Imagine that we are in the habit of consuming, say, 100 ounces of meat per week. What is the marginal utility of meat for us? To find the answer, we compare the total satisfaction we would get from consuming 100 ounces of meat per week with the total satisfaction we would get from consuming 99 ounces of meat per week, everything else unchanged. Subtracting the latter from the former, we get the marginal utility of meat for one particular consumer (ourselves) at one particular rate of meat consumption (100 ounces per week).

This concept is then employed in two propositions which form the core of the theory. First:

> There is asserted to be a "law" of *diminishing marginal utility* to the effect that as a consumer increases his rate of consumption of a particular commodity (say, from 100 to 150 ounces of meat per week) its marginal utility for him will diminish.

And second:

> It is claimed that each consumer will attempt to *maximize* his satisfactions. He will do this by spending his income on different commodities in such a way that the marginal utility he receives from spending a dollar on any one commodity will be equal to the marginal utility he receives from spending a dollar on any other commodity. Or, equivalently, he will adjust his purchases of commodities so that the ratios of their marginal utilities (for him) will be equal to the ratios of their prices.

The reasoning behind the conclusion that, in equilibrium, price ratios and marginal utility ratios will be equal may be suggested by supposing that this were *not* to be the case. A particular consumer, say, is buying potatoes and shirts to the point where their marginal utilities for him are 10 units ("utils") for one pound of potatoes and 8 units ("utils") for a shirt. Suppose that the price of potatoes is $1 per pound and that shirts cost $2 each. Could this be an equilibrium situation? The answer is *no*. For the consumer could give up one shirt (losing 8 "utils"), buy another pound of potatoes (gaining 10 "utils"), and still have a dollar left over to buy either more potatoes or some other utility-producing article. So he will start switching his expenditures from shirts to potatoes. But not indefinitely, because there is the law of diminishing marginal utility to contend with. As he buys more and more potatoes, the marginal utility of potatoes for him will decline, while the reverse is happening with shirts. Ultimately, he will reach a point where the marginal utility ratio and the price-ratio are equal. In our hypothetical example, it might be when the marginal utility of potatoes had fallen to 5 utils and the marginal utility of shirts had risen to 10 utils. At this point, the consumer will have no motive to continue switching his purchases; he will be in equilibrium.

With this line of reasoning, we can see that the *paradox of value* which had troubled Smith and Ricardo immediately loses its sting. Diamonds and gold are scarce; water and air are abundant. Although the total utility to us of water far exceeds that of diamonds, we have such an abundance of the former that its *marginal* utility becomes very, very small, even falling to zero. Diamonds, being very scarce, have a high marginal utility. Thus, there is nothing paradoxical at all about the fact that we are willing to pay more for diamonds than for water. Indeed, if we did not do so, we would be failing to maximize our total satisfactions and, in effect, behaving irrationally.

The theory thus immediately clarifies a problem that had bothered many economists. As such, it was a clear and distinct improvement over similar efforts in the past.

THE MARSHALLIAN SYNTHESIS

But was this more than a small analytic amendment? Did it merit in any way the claim of being a "revolutionary" departure? To bring out the issue most clearly, let us compare the views of the two leading British economists of the period, Alfred Marshall and William Stanley Jevons.

That these two men should have had differences of view is easily understandable, for they were quite different in temperament and also in the circumstances of their lives. Marshall died at the age of 81, the great Cambridge scholar, bearing in his last days "more than ever, the aspect of a Sage or Prophet." Jevons died at the age of 47, his life and work cut short by a swimming accident. Marshall was a great perfectionist about his work. He brooded over his theories, withholding them from publication until he had seen all their consequences and polished their written expression to the point of near perfection. In the meantime his ideas and influence were spread through the great Cambridge oral tradition. By contrast, Jevons was highly impatient. He rushed quickly into print with whatever he had and thus offered a brilliant sketch rather than a developed theory of his subject. Jevons' first writings were published while he was in college and his economics masterpiece—*Theory of Political Economy*—was written in a single year. Because of these differences in style, Jevons brought forth his version of the utility theory well before Marshall (in 1871), but his book received little immediate notice. Marshall's *Principles of Economics* did not come out until 1890, but it was an infinitely more finished work, and it was received with a **53** world-wide chorus of praise.

The two men also differed in their approach to economics. Jevons was a whole-hearted enthusiast for the new mathematical methods while Marshall—who was actually a trained mathematician and used such methods with much greater ease—felt that mathematics was best relegated to appendices and footnotes since it added little to the substance of what was being said. More important, they differed about the relationship of the new marginal analysis to earlier economic thought, especially that of the classical writers. Jevons' position was the more dramatic. He referred to Ricardo as that "able but wrong-headed man," and argued that the new analysis essentially superseded the classical position. He wrote:

> Repeated reflecton and inquiry have led me to the somewhat novel opinion, that *value depends entirely upon utility*. Prevailing opinions make labour rather than utility the origin of value; and there are even those who distinctly assert that labour is the *cause* of value. I show, on the contrary, that we have only to trace out carefully the natural laws of the variation of utility, as depending upon the quantity of commodity in our possession, in order to arrive at a satisfactory theory of exchange, of which the ordinary laws of supply and demand are a necessary consequence. This theory is in harmony with facts; and, whenever there is any apparent reason for the belief that labour is the cause of value, we obtain an explanation of the reason. Labour is found often to determine value, but only in an indirect manner, by varying the degree of utility of the commodity through an increase or limitation of the supply.

Thus, in Jevons' view, the classical analysis, insofar as it is correct, becomes a deduction from a deeper and more universal principle which the earlier writers had not understood.

Marshall, however, criticized the above statement of Jevons as "no less one-sided and fragmentary and much more misleading" than the opposite statements of Ricardo about the cost-of-production side of value. His own position was that the new utility analysis simply supplemented the earlier work on the analysis of cost:

> The "cost of production principle" and the "final [marginal] utility" principle are undoubtedly component parts of the one all-ruling law of supply and demand; each may be compared to one blade of a pair of scissors. When one blade is held still, and the cutting is effected by moving the other, we may say with careless brevity that the cutting is done by the second; but the statement is not one to be made formally, and defended deliberately.

The analogy of the scissors is used twice in Marshall's *Principles* and gives rise to what has been called the Marshallian Synthesis. By this synthesis, the classical emphasis on labor and cost-of-production and the (then) modern emphasis on utility are brought into harmony through the omnipresent law of supply and demand. If Ricardo was wrong to underemphasize utility, Jevons was almost as bad in the opposite direction—so spoke the great Marshall.

Actually, if interpreted literally, neither of the quotations above is completely satisfactory. If we take Jevons' statement that "value depends entirely upon utility" to mean that we can determine the relative prices of all commodities in the economy simply by knowing the utility functions or subjective tastes of everyone in the economy, then it is clearly wrong. To determine these prices we should also have to know something about the technology and resources of this economy. If, for example, an invention makes a particular commodity easier to produce, this will generally lower its exchange-value (in a competitive economy) even in the absence of any shift in consumer tastes.

On the other hand, Marshall's position also leaves something to be desired. For his quotation above seems to make the "cost of production principle" and the "final [marginal] utility principle" into two different principles. But it was one of the great virtues of the marginal utility analysis that it showed that "cost" could not in general be determined independently of utility considerations. Take, for example, an old problem that had bothered both Marx and Ricardo: the problem of different *qualities* of labor. Why is it that when we come to calculate the "costs" of various commodities and services we have to count one kind of labor (ditchdiggers) at $1 an hour and another kind of labor (brain surgeons) at $100 an hour? In general, the full answer cannot be given without taking into account the utilities of the commodities or services that these different kinds of labor are capable of producing. Those who tried to handle this problem without recognizing the utility element ran into endless problems.[7]

In one sense, however, it seems clear that Marshall was wise in his emphasis on continuities with the past. Economists since and including Adam Smith had been speaking of prices as somehow determined by "supply and demand." The problem had been to give a clear-cut definition of what "supply" and "demand" meant and to show how these terms were related to the underlying factors of cost and utility. Progress had been made on this matter during the middle decades of the nineteenth century (John Stuart Mill being an important contributor) but it was really during the period we are discussing here that the supply and demand apparatus came fully into its own.

Marshall himself contributed to this development in a number of ways. He emphasized the value of what is called *partial equilibrium analysis*—the analysis of the determination of price in a particular market holding all other

---

[7] Marx and Ricardo both ran afoul of this problem and attempted to handle it by regarding skilled labor as a simple multiple of average quality labor. But how does one determine the proper multiple? If, as Ricardo did, we take the multiple as given in the market place, then we are in danger of circular reasoning—taking results of our price-setting process as a basis for explaining the price-setting process. Another approach —explaining all differences in labor skills as a product of the investment of education, training, etc. in the laborer—works only if there are no inherently different qualities among men relevant to their economic potentials. Since this seems patently untrue, the only recourse ultimately is to bring in the utility side.

factors constant— and thus paved the way for the extended use of the supply and demand curves which are typically the first tools of analysis the modern student of economics encounters. He also drew sharp attention to the role of *time* in supply and demand adjustments. Marshall was fully aware that the way in which individuals, and especially business firms, are able to adjust to new economic situations will be very much influenced by the time period over which the adjustments can be made. His distinctions as to "temporary" or "long" or "short run normal" equilibrium pointed up important differences that had not been sufficiently noticed.[8]

And all this could be regarded as basically a development and refinement of ideas about supply and demand that were implicit in economic thinking quite early on. Marshall was almost certainly too generous in his specific interpretation of some of the classical writers (especially Ricardo) and rather too hard on Jevons, but the notion of late-nineteenth century analysis as a culmination or "synthesis" of previous strands of thought is not unreal when we think in terms of partial equilibrium and supply and demand analysis.

In another sense, however, there was a good deal more novelty than this might suggest. For it was through the concept of marginal utility that economists at this time—including Marshall—came to understand the full implications of the interdependence of all elements of an economic system. And this understanding, if not exactly new, was deeper than anything the classical economists had been able to achieve. The man who made the greatest contribution here was, however, neither Jevons nor Marshall; he was Léon Walras of Lausanne, Switzerland.

THE CONCEPT
OF GENERAL EQUILIBRIUM

The problem of the coherence of a competitive, unregulated, market economy is a basic one. The working of Adam Smith's "invisible hand," we recall, depends on the presumption that actual prices ("market prices") will always tend toward their equilibrium levels ("natural prices"). This is perhaps intuitively reasonable when we think of isolated commodities here and there in the economy, but when we look at the economy as a whole we are forced to ask: How can we be sure that all prices can actually *be* at their equilibrium levels at the same time? How can we be certain that a consistent over-all solution is possible? Furthermore, if "market prices" temporarily diverge from their "natural" levels, how can we be sure that they

[8] For a fuller discussion of Marshall's many contributions and for a fascinating account of the man, see "Alfred Marshall," in J. M. Keynes, *Essays in Biography* (New York: Harcourt, Brace, 1933).

will return? May not the divergence simply become greater and greater, moving the economy farther and farther away from an equilibrium position?

With a moment's reflection, it should be apparent that these are not easy questions and that their answers require something more than educated common sense. Indeed, with the posing of such questions, this part of theoretical economics began to move out of the area of general discussion and into an area where refined and sometimes quite complex techniques were required.

The necessity for a new approach was very clear to Léon Walras. He came to economics through the influence of his father, Auguste, after some rather unsatisfying ventures in engineering, journalism, and novel-writing. Because he lacked the requisite formal preparation in the field, he failed to obtain a teaching position in his native France and, for several years, he held a variety of posts—railway clerk, bank director, editor, lecturer, journalist—while his economic ideas matured. Finally, in 1870, he was appointed to an economics professorship in the Law Faculty of the University of Lausanne, Switzerland, and, four years later, the first edition of his masterpiece, *Elements of Pure Economics,* was published. Despite its great importance, the work was for many years if not overlooked at least neglected by the economics profession and, indeed, it was only in 1954 that it was finally translated into English.

The new approach was, in essence, mathematical.[9] Walras had none of Marshall's reservations about the use of mathematics in economics and, indeed, he felt that non-mathematical persons had no future in theoretical economics. Such economists, Walras wrote, "will always have to face the alternative either of steering clear of this discipline and consequently elaborating a theory of applied economics without recourse to a theory of pure economics or of tackling the problems of pure economics without the necessary equipment, thus producing not only very bad pure economics but also very bad mathematics." Economists *with* mathematics, on the other hand, had every reason to have great hopes for the future. For Walras was confident that, one day, "mathematical economics will rank with the mathematical sciences of astronomy and mechanics" and on that day, he concludes, "justice will be done to our work."

Since Walras conceived economic method in this particular way, his *Elements* is in form very different from such other masterpieces as the *Wealth of Nations, Capital,* Ricardo's *Principles of Political Economy* and even Alfred Marshall's *Principles.* Marshall was always very eager that his work should

---

[9] We use the term "new approach" loosely for there was a long line of economists before Walras who, in greater or lesser degree, had seen the possibilities of mathematical economics. If we had to select one of these for special reference, it should probably be Augustin Cournot who, as early as 1838, published an important work in mathematical economics, his *Researches into the Mathematical Principles of the Theory of Wealth.*

be read and understood by businessmen, but it would have been a rare businessman who took on Walras! He begins by defining his problem in a narrow and highly abstract way. "Pure economics" (he writes) "is, in essence, the theory of the determination of prices under a hypothetical regime of perfectly free competition." The book then builds in a succession of stages—exchange of two commodities, exchange of several commodities, theory of production, and so on—to a system of simultaneous equations by which, in principle, all unknown prices and quantities in the system can be solved.

The picture of the economy that emerges from this treatment may be described roughly as follows.[10] Assume that we have a freely competitive economy and that fundamental conditions—consumer tastes, technology, quantities of land, labor and capital—remain unchanged. Envisage this economy as divided into two great markets: (1) a product market and (2) a factor market. In the first market, the sellers are largely business firms who have produced the goods being sold and the buyers are largely consuming households. In the second market, the business firms are now the buyers while the sellers are the households who own the labor, land, and other factors of production.

What happens in the Walrasian system—in more complex form of course—is that the buyers and sellers go to their respective markets, each guided by the desire to maximize his utility. Various prices and quantities are offered until an over-all equilibrium is reached. This equilibrium is characterized by two conditions:

(a) no party can increase his utility by any change in his own actions;
(b) the total quantity of each commodity and each productive service demanded is exactly equal to that supplied.

Walras then shows that, in general, a determinate solution to this problem can be found, demonstrating that "the number of equations entailed is exactly equal to the number of unknowns." This, in barest outline, is what is known as a system of *general equilibrium*.

To understand what such a system involves, however, it is necessary to see how it displays the over-all interdependence of economic phenomena. To do this, let us go back to the example we used in the case of Adam Smith of a change in the demand for cotton-cloth. We can now take into account two elements we glossed over earlier: the effect of a change in the demand for one commodity on the demand for other commodities, and the effect of these changes in demand on the prices of the factors of production.

We imagine a two-commodity world: cotton-cloth and wheat are its

[10] It should be pointed out that the following discussion of general equilibrium theory is necessarily very fragmentary. The student with a good mathematical background who wishes to pursue this matter at length may consult Robert E. Kuenne, *The Theory of General Economic Equilibrium* (Princeton: Princeton University Press, 1963).

only products. We suppose further that there are only two factors of production, labor and land, and that wheat production uses (relatively) a great deal of land and little labor and that cloth production uses (relatively) a great deal of labor and little land. If the demand for wheat rises relatively to cloth, then:

> In the first instance, wheat prices will rise relatively to cloth prices. This change in relative prices will make it profitable for producers to shift from cloth to wheat production. However, since wheat production uses relatively more land and relatively less labor, the shifting from cloth to wheat will mean a general rise in the demand for land and a general decline in the demand for labor. Assuming that the amounts of land and labor available to the economy are fixed, this rise in demand for land and decline in demand for labor will lead to a rise in the price of land relative to labor. This rise in the relative price of land will have two effects: (a) it will change the distribution of income between laborers and landowners in favor of the latter; and (b) it will make it profitable for producers to substitute wherever possible the now cheaper labor for the now more expensive land in the production of *both* wheat and cloth. The final equilibrium which is likely to result in this case therefore will involve: (1) increased wheat production; (2) decreased cloth production; (3) higher price of wheat relative to the price of cloth; (4) higher price of land relative to the price of labor; (5) greater incomes for landowners relative to laborers; and (6) greater use of labor relative to land in the production of both wheat and cloth.

What we have shown here is how a change in one part of the economy—in this case a change in consumer tastes—can lead to changes throughout the economic system. The exchange value of the commodities has changed (wheat is now more expensive), the manner of producing commodities has changed (labor has been in some degree substituted for land), and the distribution of income in the society has been changed (in favor of the landowners). In the analysis of general equilibrium, the problems of value, production, and distribution become simply aspects of one integrated view of the entire economic process.

Thus, although economic theory in the late-nineteenth century may have narrowed the range of problems under consideration, nevertheless within that range it presented a truly *comprehensive* analysis of economic phenomena. And it was this, far more than the concept of marginal utility in itself, that made possible the claims of a "revolutionary" advance.

EVALUATION AND CRITICISM

This description of the accomplishments of late-nineteenth century economic theory may make it easier to understand why the work of this period has been widely praised and roundly criticized by subsequent writers.

As far as criticisms are concerned, they have differed greatly in scope and depth. Some critics have directed themselves to the basic framework of nineteenth-century analysis. They have charged that the theory is based on ridiculously simplistic assumptions about human behavior and economic institutions. Where, they ask, do we find the kind of person envisaged in the theory, this "rational maximizer of utility," this purely "economic man"? Where, for that matter, do we find the kind of freely competitive markets wherein prices are set impersonally by the forces of supply and demand? Does this have anything to do with the realities of modern capitalism?

These questions are really part of an over-all charge that, by narrowing and simplifying too much, late-nineteenth century economics succeeded in omitting most of the truly important questions about the workings of a modern economy. They had little or nothing to say (at least in their formal theories) about big business, big labor, big government. They largely ignored the growth process both within and as affecting capitalistic institutions. They added very little to our knowledge of the cause of unemployment and depressions. Some of the matters which the twentieth century has come to consider *central* to economics, these writers barely touched at all.

Such criticisms are important and valid and, indeed, the subsequent chapters of this book will be concerned to show how economics in the twentieth century has attempted (successfully in some cases; not so successfully in others) to improve the tools and broaden the scope of the subject so that it can cope with these neglected problems.

But criticism has not been directed solely at the basic framework of the late-nineteenth century analysis; it has also involved criticism of important assumptions made *within* that framework. For although the work of this period brought a new precision to the analysis of the problems on which it focused, it did not always solve them in a completely satisfactory way. One obvious difficulty concerned the concept of marginal utility itself. The theories of Marshall, Jevons, Walras, Menger and, indeed, most of the writers of this period, posited the existence of quantitatively measurable utility. The consumer is in equilibrium in our earlier example when, the price of a shirt being $2 and the price of a pound of potatoes being $1, the marginal utilities of these commodities to him are 10 "utils" and 5 "utils" respectively. But can we actually provide a satisfactory numerical measure of a consumer's psychological state? Isn't this allegedly scientific theory based on a will-o'-the-wisp?

In point of fact, this particular criticism did not prove as damaging to the over-all structure of late-nineteenth century theory as might be expected. Beginning with Walras' successor at Lausanne—the eminent Italian scientist, economist and sociologist, Vilfredo Pareto (1848-1923)—and continuing on with numerous contemporary contributors such as Oxford University's J. R. Hicks, economists have shown that general equilibrium theory can be constructed without assuming a quantitatively measurable utility. Modern economics uses a theory of consumer preference in which the consumer is asked if he "prefers" one set of goods to another (or is "indifferent" as between them), not by *how much* he prefers them.[11]

And, indeed, this example suggests some of the underlying virtues of late-nineteenth century analysis. For the fact is that this analysis has proved to be well-adapted to improvement and thus essentially very durable. Large parts of present-day economic theory can be shown to be directly derivative from the work of this period. Probably the most important technical contribution lay in the development of the tools of what we can call *marginal analysis.* The particular concept of marginal utility may have gone by the board, but in its place there are marginal rates of substitution, marginal products, marginal costs, marginal revenues, marginal rates of transformation and a host of other such terms which are at the very core of economic theory today.[12]

Beyond this, there was the great vision of the interdependence of economic life. Instead of having a theory of value, and then another theory of production, and possibly still another theory of distribution, the economists of this period showed explicitly how all these aspects of economic activity are related to each other and, how, moreover, they form in total a coherent and unified whole.

At this point, we may ask one final question about late-nineteenth century thought. If the economists of this period showed that pure competition was a consistent system, did they also show that it was the "best possible" system? The fundamental point about Adam Smith's "invisible hand," after all, was that private forces under competitive conditions would lead to the welfare of society. How did this conclusion stand up in terms of the now much more precise and penetrating analysis of a competitive economy?

The answer to this question is a complicated one and, indeed, the subject of what is called *welfare economics* has become one of the most intricate (and ofttimes frustrating) branches of twentieth-century economic thought. Suffice it to say here that while the new analysis provided a more rigorous basis for Adam Smith's conclusion, it also changed the meaning of that con-

---

[11] This change has meant, of course, that consumer equilibrium can no longer be expressed by saying that price ratios are equal to the ratios of marginal utilities. The modern equivalent is that price ratios are equal to the relevant "marginal rates of substitution." This latter refers to the amount of one commodity which must be given to the consumer to replace one unit of another commodity in order that the consumer shall be just as "well off" as before. For a much more detailed treatment of this matter see, in this Series, Robert Dorfman, *Prices and Markets,* and also Chapter 3 of Dorfman's *The Price System.*

[12] The mathematically inclined reader will recognize all these "marginal" terms as essentially derivatives. The marginal product of labor, for example, is the partial derivative of total product with respect to labor. This part of economic theory, today, is virtually all expressed in mathematical terms in more advanced studies.

clusion and considerably narrowed its range of applicability. The essential drift of the new analysis may be expressed as follows:

> Pure competition has, under many circumstances, certain "ideal" properties. However, it must be kept in mind: (a) that the distribution of income as resulting from "natural" forces may be good, bad, or indifferent— i.e., the establishment of pure competition does not in any way guarantee a desirable distribution of income; and (b) that there exist certain definite situations in which it can be shown that private and social interest diverge under a regime of unregulated competition.

Needless to say, a complex, qualified statement of this sort does not provide the kind of rallying-cry which the doctrine of *laissez-faire* provided in an earlier age. And, in point of fact, economists of the modern day have found it possible to accept such a statement and yet to move in quite different ideological directions. Some have stressed the "ideal" properties of a competitive market economy; others have stressed the overriding importance of those areas in which private and social interest diverge.

We shall be indicating some of these different directions in the remaining chapters before us. For the moment we note only that the force and simplicity of the late-eighteenth century defense of an unregulated market economy was, in the late-nineteenth century, being subjected to qualifications. To some this will seem unfortunate. But, in reality, it is only the price that must be paid when intuition—however brilliant—gives way to actual analysis.

SUMMARY

Economic analysis in the late-nineteenth century became more narrow, precise, and professional. The key concept was *utility,* and especially *marginal utility*. The theory of marginal utility was anticipated by many writers and developed simultaneously and independently by a number of others—such as Menger, Walras, Jevons, and Marshall. The theory solved a number of difficulties inherent in a cost or labor approach to value theory (e.g., the *paradox of value*) and offered a stepping-stone to the theory of *general equilibrium* formulated in essentially mathematical terms.

Marshall considered that the new theory simply complemented the earlier achievements of the classical economists, and the Marshallian synthesis with its explication of supply and demand analysis and its conjoining of the forces of cost and utility does represent a fairly continuous development of earlier themes. For Jevons and Walras, however, a "revolution" in theoretical economics was taking place, and this revolution was typified more than anything else by Walras' brilliant and explicit statement of the coherence and interdependence of a competitive economy.

Subsequent critics have attacked the narrowness of range of late-nineteenth century economics and even some of its concepts, such as marginal utility. However, *within* its range, this theory did represent a far more comprehensive statement of the workings of a competitive economy than had ever been offered before. Furthermore, and partly because of its mathematical methods, this theory has proved quite durable. Its basic structure has survived the elimination even of what was once its key concept—quantitatively measurable marginal utility—and it remains, despite further modifications that we shall take up presently, an integral part of modern economic theory.

Institutions, Innovations,

and Imperfections

By the beginning of the twentieth century, mainstream economics had to its credit a theoretical structure that was insightful, simple, and highly systematic. General equilibrium analysis represented a remarkable effort at generalization in a field of knowledge that was still young by historical standards. It remains to this day one of the great intellectual achievements of the modern social sciences.

But it also had its limitations. As we have said, late-nineteenth century analysis dealt largely with a purely competitive, static, full employment world—a world such as never existed, and certainly not at the turn of the century. Consider the American economy at that time. It was a vibrant, vital, growing economy. The great railroad construction, population growth, and westward expansion of the post-Civil War period had created a huge national market in which nothing was static. The economy was full of imperfections. It was the age of the great promoter, of "captains of industry"— men like Cornelius Vanderbilt, J. Pierpont Morgan, Jim Fisk, Jay Gould, John D. Rockefeller. The establishment of the United States Steel Corporation was, in its way, a dramatic exemplar of the trends of the times. Far from being a small competitive firm responding to the impersonal dictates of the market, this was an economic mammoth dominating one of the largest and most vital industries of an expanding modern economy. It was also a bloated mammoth, for, against its actual assets of less than $700 million, there had been sold stocks and bonds to the value of over $1.3 billion—an

65

overvaluation that brought millions upon millions of dollars of profits to its sponsors.

What did competitive general equilibrium theory have to say about this? Indeed, what relevance did the whole of standard economic analysis have to the world of affairs as anyone who glanced at the newspapers knew it actually to be?

In this chapter and the next, we shall consider the attempts of economists in the first half of the twentieth century to bring a greater realism to the structure of economic theory. Some of these economists completely rejected traditional theory; others sought only to modify it; still others ranged somewhere in between. Their common bond was the conviction that there existed an undesirable gap between economic theory and economic reality which must somehow be removed.

In this chapter, we shall consider three criticisms from the early decades of the century: those of Thorstein Veblen, Joseph A. Schumpeter, and the writers of the imperfect-monopolistic competition school.

INSTITUTIONS: THE SWEEPING CRITIQUE
OF THORSTEIN VEBLEN

The most radical of the criticisms undoubtedly was that of Thorstein Veblen (1857-1929). This aloof, skeptical, phrase-making American economist-sociologist wished to recast the whole of economic analysis so that real-life motives and institutions and their evolution over time would form the core of its subject matter.

Veblen stood apart from the mainstream of economic thought and, in many ways, standing apart was the characteristic posture of his life. He was the son of Norwegian immigrant parents, born in Wisconsin and brought up on a farm in Minnesota as one of a family of nine children. His relationship with the academic profession—which he later castigated in his discussions of the "higher learning"—was distinctly ambiguous. In the course of his life he wrote ten books and numerous articles and was a widely acclaimed figure on the American intellectual scene, but he never was able to settle into a satisfactory academic post. His early efforts to find jobs at the University of Iowa and St. Olaf's failed. At the University of Chicago, where he taught for many years, he rose no higher than an assistant professorship. After Chicago, he taught at Stanford, the University of Missouri, held a minor government post during World War I, and then went on to the New School for Social Research—a perpetual wanderer in the groves of academe. Nor is this difficult to understand. For Veblen was iconoclastic, irreverent, a bearded, bespectacled, oddly dressed man, who, however, inspired a certain responsiveness in the hearts of his feminine students and thus gave further uneasiness to the universities which employed him. But it was characteristic that he should thus stand back from the accepted and conventional mode of life. He viewed the culture of his time with a critical, distrustful eye, liking nothing better than to spike with a sharply ironic phrase the reputable beliefs that most of his contemporaries held dear.

Veblen's most famous book—*The Theory of the Leisure Class*—was his first, published in 1899 when he was forty-two. Many of the ideas introduced at this time were further developed in a number of books, published during the first decades of the twentieth century, on the price system, business enterprise, the "instinct" of workmanship, and farther afield, a history of Imperial Germany. His writing has certain curious qualities to it, not the least being his habit of saying that it is not his purpose to evaluate but simply to analyze and then his proceeding to give a completely devastating evaluation of the matter at hand. In *The Theory of the Leisure Class,* he writes: "The only class which could at all dispute with the hereditary leisure class the honour of an habitual bellicose frame of mind is that of the lower class delinquents." A member of the upper classes would hardly be likely to take this as objective reporting. Though, in another sense, it *is* objective, since Veblen had a serious theory to explain the similarities between the very wealthy and the delinquent classes.

The range of subject matter is extremely wide, and at times a bit surprising. What other economist has ever devoted extended attention to the "corset" considered from the point of view of "economic theory"? [1] And this range is not incidental but central to Veblen's approach. For what he is interested in is not the formal properties of consumer preference and the market system but the habits of mind that influence economic behavior and how these habits have developed and are likely to change.

Specifically, he makes the following criticisms of the economic doctrines of the period:

1. *Utility Theory:* He rejects the concept of economic man as a rational maximizer of utility, or, as he puts it, "a lightning calculator of pleasures and pains, who oscillates like a homogeneous globule of desire of happiness under the impulse of stimuli that shift him about the area, but leave him intact." Such a version of human behavior he believes is not only bad psychology but hopelessly uninformative.

2. *Consumer Behavior:* He finds traditional theory useless for dealing with consumers as they actually are. According to Veblen, the striking feature of modern consumers is their desire to prove their superior reputability to their fellows. Consumption is not primarily to satisfy material wants—indus-

[1] The "corset" is important in Veblen as an illustration of the way in which people prove that they do not have to work—an indulgence in what he calls "conspicuous leisure." Thus, "the corset is, in economic theory, substantially a mutilation, undergone for the purpose of lowering the subject's vitality and rendering her permanently and obviously unfit for work."

trial civilization has created a great margin over subsistence for all classes, especially the upper classes—but is a vehicle for making "invidious" distinctions between persons and classes. Modern man indulges in "conspicuous consumption," "conspicuous leisure," and "conspicuous waste." If the husband is engaged in work, he has his wife indulge in "vicarious consumption" for him. Dress, sports, religion, humanistic education—all have as a main function the demonstration of superior status.

3. *Business Behavior:* He also rejects the traditional figure of the efficient, competitive businessman. The businessman in Veblen's world is ignorant of industrial processes and wholly engaged in pecuniary manipulations and "capitalistic sabotage." Veblen traces the true ancestry of the great promoters back to the predatory spirit of the barbarian. His businessman makes profits not by giving effect to the forces of industrialization but by deranging them—holding back production to keep prices high, engaging in credit transactions that bring on crises, constantly interfering with the work of his technology-minded engineers.

4. *An Evolutionary Economics:* Veblen wants his economics dynamic and evolutionary, not static. In this, he was much influenced by Darwinian thought and, to some degree, by Marx. He agrees with Marx to the extent of arguing that the economic-technological factor is of vast importance in the modern industrial age. The great force making for change is what he calls the "machine process." The development of machines has not only made possible a different standard of life compared to times past but has outmoded many of the traditional institutions and habits of thought that man has carried forward from his barbarian origins.

5. *Economic and Social Classes:* Again like Marx, Veblen rejects any simplistic notion of the harmony of private and social interest and, specifically, finds the interest of the businessman opposed to the welfare of the community. But his views on social classes are ultimately non-Marxian. For Veblen, the struggle between business and labor is not crucial and is really a game "played between two contending interests for private gain." The much more serious conflict is between, on the one hand, the businessman, who makes money, and, on the other hand, the technologists and engineers, who actually make the goods. Indeed, it is ultimately broader than that, because Veblen recognizes that class demarcations are by no means fixed and that the attitudes of one class shade into those of another and constantly interact. The *real* conflict is between two habits of mind: the one—exemplified in the spirit of business enterprise—is anachronistic, predatory, a carry-over from the anthropologically distant past; the other—deriving from the machine process—is matter-of-fact, scientific, given to the objective analysis of cause and effect. It is this conflict between the modern and the archaic which gives the characteristic flavor of discord and maladjustment to the world of Thorstein Veblen. It is also this conflict that makes his world seem so much more vigorous and

life-like than the pale, often rather abstract, maximizing world of traditional theory.[2]

But what does it all add up to? It is one thing to criticize and another to build a positive and systematic theory to replace what has been abandoned. On the whole Veblen is better as skeptic and critic than as builder, though there is in his work the unifying theme of the discord between technology and anachronistic institutions, and, occasionally, he even goes so far as to suggest the future outcome of this battle. As might be expected, he sees in the future the gradual extension of the machine process to wider and wider reaches of modern life. In one of his later publications, *The Engineers and the Price System* (1921), he suggests that there is some evidence that the technologists are becoming "class-conscious" and are beginning to recognize that "they together constitute the indispensable general staff of the industrial system." He does not rule out the possibility that this group might one day engage in outright collective action against their natural enemies, the businessmen. He writes:

> And there is the patent fact that such a thing as a general strike of the technological specialists in industry need involve no more than a minute fraction of one per cent of the population; yet it would swiftly bring a collapse of the old order and sweep the timeworn fabric of finance and absentee sabotage into the discard for good and all.

Veblen hedges his prediction somewhat but the basic drift of things seems fairly plain to him. The engineers and technologists, representing the machine process and, ultimately, the welfare of the community, hold in their hands the trump-cards of evolution. Should they ever realize their strength, the pecuniary, predatory, commercial world of business enterprise will fade into the past. Nor—despite his claim to objectivity—can we imagine that this is a consummation to which Veblen himself would have offered much objection!

This theory was clearly far outside the mainstream of economic thought at the time it was written. And, to some extent, this is still true. Present-day students of economics in this country typically read Veblen as they read Marx —that is, as an example of interesting, far-reaching views which happen to be quite different from their own.

Still, Veblen has had an influence on the evolution of modern economics in a variety of ways. For one thing, a number of his specific ideas have become part of the background of modern discussions and, in some cases, have been incorporated into systematic theories of the economic process. The concept of "conspicuous consumption," with its emphasis on the social character of con-

---

[2] One of the penalties of the high degree of generalization achieved by theoretical economics in the late-nineteenth century was that the concept of social and economic classes, so vivid in Marx and, if not vivid, at least discernible in classical economics, tended to disappear from economic theory. The natural tendency of abstract general equilibrium theory is to deal not with business and labor, or the landlord and the capitalist, but with the owners of m factors of production, producing n products. There is a great gain in generality in this procedure, but sometimes there is a loss in content.

sumption decisions and the interdependence of consumer choices, has proved important and durable. So also has his recognition of the fact that while consumers quickly adjust to a higher standard of living, they strongly resist any encroachment upon their habitual standard when incomes are falling. His discussion of technology and the machine-process needs only the addition of words like "automation" and "computerization" to have a distinctly modern flavor.

For another thing, he influenced a number of particular American economists, some of whom are roughly classed with him as forming the *institutionalist school* of economics. His most eminent student and admirer was Wesley Clair Mitchell (1874-1948) who, although of a very different temperament, nevertheless was impressed by many of his teacher's criticisms of orthodox theory. Mitchell's great accomplishments were in empirical and statistical research, particularly in the field of business cycles. He founded the National Bureau of Economic Research in 1920, an organization which to this day has brought forth countless monographs on the quantitative aspects of economic phenomena.

But perhaps Veblen's greatest influence, though subtle and indirect, has been one of tone. At a time when many pure theorists were congratulating themselves on the "revolution" in economic theory, Veblen weighed in with a healthy load of satire and skepticism. He pointed out how shallow were the simplifying assumptions which economists, bent on systematic theorization, were in the habit of using. Even today, it is impossible to read Veblen without realizing how many important questions economic theory still cannot answer, how far the science must go before all the essential features of economic reality are captured. This, of course, is a largely negative achievement. But, for all that, it is not an unimportant one.

INNOVATIONS: JOSEPH A. SCHUMPETER
AND THE THEORY OF GROWTH

If Veblen called for a major re-writing of economic theory, so also did Joseph Alois Schumpeter (1883-1950), the Austrian-born and later Harvard economist whose name we have already had occasion to mention.[3] There was this difference, however. Whereas Veblen rejected late-nineteenth century theory, Schumpeter had a keen appreciation of its virtues and, indeed, used it explicitly as his point of departure.

---

[3] As author of an outstanding history of economic thought (see above, p. 47). For those who, like the present author, studied under Schumpeter, his influence is deep in many different directions. Stories about him still fill the air in Cambridge, Massachusetts. His grading (to take one example) was notoriously easy. It is said that Schumpeter always gave A's to (a) all female students; (b) all Chinese students; and (c) all other students. He was a remarkable and increasingly legendary figure.

It can be argued that Schumpeter should be discussed at the end of this book—not here among early twentieth-century economists. Schumpeter was still producing interesting work during and after World War II and many of his ideas had their greatest impact on the post-war generation. However, it seems preferable to treat his work now because his seminal masterpiece, The *Theory of Economic Development,* was published in 1911 and its central "vision" had been worked out by 1909, when, incidentally, Schumpeter was a ripe twenty-six years old! Actually, Schumpeter had a theory about this matter. It was his view that a man's truly creative period was almost invariably the third decade of his life. There are probably some exceptions to this generalization; but it does fit Schumpeter's own performance remarkably well.

This performance begins, in the *Theory of Economic Development,* with a particular restatement of general equilibrium theory. Schumpeter imagines a competitive economy in a condition of stationary equilibrium. There is movement in this economy but no change in fundamental conditions. There is a "circular flow" of goods and services in one direction and money in the opposite direction. Producers use money to buy the services of the factors of production who, in turn, as consumers, use the money to buy the goods which the producers employing the factors of production have produced. This "circular flow" is, *ex hypothesi,* the same every year. There is no saving or net additional investment in capital goods. There are no changes in methods of production. Everything goes on in one period as it did in the previous period, and the standard equilibrium conditions—such as that the relative prices of all goods must be equal to the ratios of their marginal utilities for each consumer —prevail and do not change over time.[4]

Schumpeter's interest in this particular picture of the economy, however, is not as a description of economic reality but as a device for isolating the causes of those aspects of reality which seem to him crucial. Those crucial aspects in the case of modern industrial capitalism can really be summed up in one word: growth! It is Schumpeter's characteristic view that all the vital phenomena of an industrial economy—business cycles, credit creation, industrial structure, even the sociological character of capitalism itself—are intimately related to the growth process. Leaving the latter out, he remarks in a later work, is "like *Hamlet* without the Danish prince."

Having established to his own satisfaction the conditions of a stationary economy, Schumpeter now asks in effect: How does growth intrude and what are its consequences?

To explain the appearance of growth, Schumpeter calls sharp attention to a function that had received relatively little analysis heretofore. The

[4] Schumpeter's discussion of the stationary competitive state would not win approval from modern economists in all particulars. For example, Schumpeter argued that in such a state the rate of interest in the economy would be zero, whereas most economists would argue that it would be low but positive. Such criticisms, however, do not much affect the central thrust—the "vision" (to use one of his favorite words)— behind Schumpeter's reasoning.

function is *innovation,* and the personage who is responsible for innovating is called the *entrepreneur.*

What precisely is an *innovation?* The essential notion is the introduction of a *new* way of utilizing the productive resources of the economy, as contrasted with the essentially routine task of managing those resources in customary ways. Schumpeter has a very broad definition in mind covering such various *new* activities as introducing new kinds of consumer goods, trying out untested methods of production, opening up new markets, finding new sources of raw materials, reorganizing the structure of a particular industry, and so on. Economic activity is essentially divided into two broad compartments: (1) administering a given structure—the central problem in the "circular flow"; and (2) creating new structures—the central problem in economic "development."

The person who innovates is, as we have said, the *entrepreneur,* though this phraseology can be misleading since a given person may combine several distinct economic functions. The essential point is that in addition to the usual productive functions involved in owning and providing the means of production there is this additional function of combining the means of production in new ways. For a century and a half, economic theory had distinguished the laborer, the landowner, and the capitalist—now the entrepreneur must be added. In particular, according to Schumpeter, his role must be sharply distinguished from that of the capitalist. It may be helpful but it is not essential for the entrepreneur to be able to supply his own capital and, in fact, being able to do so has nothing to do with his essential function. The *pure* type of entrepreneur is penniless. He must go to the bank and borrow the wherewithal he needs to get started on his new project. Indeed, convincing the banker is only one of several obstacles that the entrepreneur must face as he attempts the harrowing task of breaking through traditional modes of behavior and hurling himself forward into the unknown.

Once the innovating entrepreneur has been introduced, Schumpeter argues, economic growth in its characteristic modern form can now take place. This characteristic form he describes with the wonderfully evocative phrase— "creative destruction." The developmental process in its essence involves a constant and deep-rooted competition between new ways of doing things and the old. In this process the old is ultimately destroyed but the consequence of its destruction is that the economy is raised to a higher level. The real competitor for a stagecoach-producer is not another stagecoach-producer but the railroad magnate. The railroad in its turn comes to face its real competition in the automobile, truck, and plane. Today's innovation replaces yesterday's and tomorrow is itself replaced. And this, in Schumpeter's view, is what growth —and the essence of modern capitalism—is all about.

Given this general picture, Schumpeter developed its implications in many different directions. Much of his attention, for example, was given to economic fluctuations, and his two-volume *Business Cycles* (1939) is a monumental, if not altogether satisfactory, attempt to put historical and statistical flesh on his theories. Characteristically, Schumpeter regarded the business cycle as inseparable from the growth process. More than that, he directly related these fluctuations to the innovational activities of entrepreneurs. The upswing begins when some entrepreneur breaks through the prevailing equilibrium with a new innovation. His success and example are quickly emulated by other quasi-entrepreneurs who follow in a swarm. Bank credit is expanded to meet the new demands; there is bidding for the factors of production; prices rise. The downswing sets in when these new innovations begin to release a flood of goods on the market and when at the same time loans are being repaid and bank credit contracted. Fundamentally, this recession in the economy is its way of absorbing the fruits of innovational advance. Presently a new equilibrium is restored, but at a higher level of national income, and the economy rests until another round of innovations initiates further fluctuation—and further progress.[5]

But Schumpeter by no means confined his analysis to business cycles. Two important examples will indicate the wide-ranging character of his thought.

The first has to do with the problem of monopolies and monopolistic elements in the economy:

> As always, Schumpeter related this problem to that of long-run growth. The characteristic view of economists—from Adam Smith to Thorstein Veblen—about monopolies was that they represented harmful, restrictive deviations from an ideal, usually purely competitive, norm. Schumpeter admitted that such deviations did occur and that they did have certain unfortunate effects when viewed from a purely short-run point of view. However, he argued that the matter looked very different when approached from a longer-run vantage. *First,* the constant competition of new products against the old—the heart of the process of "creative destruction"—means that all firms, even apparent monopolies, are subject to pressures which severely limit the range within which they may exploit the consumer. *Second,* given the uncertainties of this growth process, a proper rate of innovation requires that firms be able to protect themselves to at least some degree. The arguments which people use to justify patents for new processes can, Schumpeter claims, be extended to cover in one degree or another most phases of industrial activity. These points, if they do not constitute a complete defense

---

[5] This is necessarily a very abbreviated version of Schumpeter's theory of the business cycle. At least two further points should be noted: (1) In addition to the fundamental cycle with its direct relationship to innovations, Schumpeter recognized the existence of a "secondary wave" of speculative activities built around the basic cycle and intensifying many of its observable characteristics. (2) Schumpeter also felt that there was not one but probably three basic business cycles. Of special interest is his view that, in addition to a short-run inventory cycle and the regular 8-10 year cycle, there was a pattern of "long waves" of anywhere from 50 to 60 years in duration. These "waves" he related to very basic innovations which took a long time for their full ramifications to be worked out—e.g., steam power, the railroad, later the automotive, electrical, and chemical industries. The existence of long waves of various durations is by no means established, but it continues to intrigue some economists to this day.

of monopoly power, nevertheless clearly put the subject into a different area of discussion.[6]

The second example has to do with the future—really the future demise —of capitalism. Schumpeter was ultimately a deep admirer of the capitalistic system but he was very pessimistic about its future, again for reasons having to do with the long-run growth process:

> Schumpeter believed that the capitalistic system was not likely to survive in the distant future. This was not because he foresaw any failure of the economic mechanism of capitalism but—paradoxically—because the system was so successful! How could success spell the demise of the system? Take the entrepreneur, the characteristic figure of the capitalistic system in Schumpeter's view. As capitalistic growth proceeds over time, the economy becomes adjusted to the process. Growth becomes not a wrenching of the old order, but an expected, ordinary phenomenon. But this is nothing else than to say that the specific function of the entrepreneur—to break away from traditional ways into new paths—becomes less and less important. The entrepreneurial function becomes routinized, obsolete. When this begins to happen, the way is clear for reformers and intellectuals to demand "improvements" in the system. And the net effect of the continuing modifications of the system will be its gradual replacement by another. Schumpeter describes this process vividly in his fascinating book, *Capitalism, Socialism and Democracy* (1942), and there gives his opinion—but not his preference —that the "heir apparent" to capitalism will be some form of socialism.

These examples indicate how Schumpeter developed from certain early insights a broad and panoramic view of the economic process, a view which ultimately spilled over into history, sociology, and political science. Of twentieth-century economists—with the possible exception of Veblen—there is probably no one who approaches him in terms of range and scope of outlook.

How then do we measure his achievement for our purposes—that is, in terms of his influence on the evolution of modern economics? Schumpeter once said that he had had three great ambitions in life—to be a great horseman, a great lover, and a great economist—and that two of these ambitions had been achieved. Certainly he was a great economist and, beyond that, a deep and stimulating thinker generally. Nevertheless, the immediate impact of his ideas on economic thought was somewhat less than might have been expected.

One reason for this was circumstance. At the time when the economics profession might have attended to his teaching, particularly during the 1930's,

---

[6] Schumpeter's theory would, in general, lead us to expect a positive correlation between firm size and the rate of innovation in a given industry. The empirical evidence on this matter is fairly inconclusive, but it is evident that Schumpeter's hypothesis is not without exceptions. See, for example, the recent study of innovation in the steel industry where the *lagging behind* of the big firms is stressed (Walter Adams and Joel B. Dirlam, "Big Steel, Invention and Innovation," *Quarterly Journal of Economics,* May, 1966). As a spur to re-thinking traditional views, however, Schumpeter's approach in this area—as in most areas—has been invaluable.

it was engrossed by a quite different kind of problem and by a revolutionary theory addressed to that problem. This was the time of the Great Depression and the "new economics" of John Maynard Keynes, matters which we shall take up in the next chapter. In a very real sense, Keynes stole Schumpeter's thunder; nor was Schumpeter unaware of this fact, as his highly critical comments on Keynes' theory attest. But the point is that in the face of an acute short-run crisis—a virtual breakdown of the economic system—economists had little interest in the more leisurely problems of long-run growth.

Another reason, however, has to do with the nature of his theory itself. For although Schumpeter developed the implications of his insights for many different areas of economic theory, he never constructed a complete and formal theoretical model to give those insights systematic expression. We have remarked before that, in economics, insight is only part of the matter and that another, and sometimes the more difficult, part is to incorporate those insights into consistent and self-contained theories. Apparently, small departures *systematically developed* often have far more impact than radical new approaches which lack such development. Of course, Schumpeter did go part of the way in this direction—much further, for example, than Veblen. He saw the merits of general equilibrium theory and made an attempt to show its relationship to his own theoretical construction. But he never succeeded in going the whole way. Or perhaps, as some of his occasional comments seem to suggest, he *preferred* not to do this, recognizing the damage to realism which every effort at "model-building" necessarily involves.

Nevertheless, Schumpeter was not altogether without influence in his own time and that influence has, on the whole, tended to increase. Present-day economics has become deeply involved in the analysis of long-run growth, and this development places Schumpeter in the role of an important anticipator of the future course of the subject. For he understood with exceptional clarity that growth is a pervasive feature of modern industrial life and that its economic consequences are new products, new methods, new advances, all contributing to higher and higher standards of living, not just for the capitalists or the entrepreneurs or any other particular group, but for the whole of society. Looking back now over the history of the industrial economies during the past century and a half, it is difficult to see how anyone could have started off from any other premise. But most economists did, and the fact that Schumpeter was so clear-sighted in this regard is a proper basis for the recognition that is now coming to him.

IMPERFECTIONS:

CHAMBERLIN, ROBINSON, AND OTHERS

Of the various departures from traditional assumptions which took place in the first third of the twentieth century, the one which probably had the most direct and immediate impact on economic theory is the last one we shall consider in this chapter. It concerns the development of new theories of what are alternatively called *monopolistic* or *imperfect competition.*[7]

This particular departure was very different in tone and character from those we have just been discussing. If Veblen wished to scrap the basic premises of traditional theory and Schumpeter wished to focus central attention on a different problem, the main feature of this new departure was the degree to which it accepted the conventionally defined problems and the conventional methods of approaching them. It was a departure that developed *out of* mainstream economic thought, not as a revolutionary protest against it, and it brought forth no ideas that would have been shocking, say, to Alfred Marshall. Though, as we have just finished saying in the last section, it is not always the largest changes that count most.

Since this departure was a natural development from what had gone before, it is understandable that not one but several economists were associated with it. In the *Economic Journal* of December 1926, Piero Sraffa (b. 1898), an Italian-born Cambridge University economist, published an important article which suggested the need for blending the separate theories of monopoly and competition. The following year, a Harvard University graduate student, Edward H. Chamberlin (b. 1899), submitted as his doctoral dissertation an extensive discussion of the same subject which was published in 1933 under the title *Monopolistic Competition.* Later that same year, working independently of Chamberlin, another Cambridge University economist, Joan Robinson (b. 1903), published a somewhat similar book, *The Economics of Imperfect Competition.* Interestingly, in the case of all three authors, the work was done in Schumpeter's precious third decade.[8]

What, then, was the new theory and what has been its lasting influence on the development of modern economics?

We have noted already that the late-nineteenth century analysis of the price mechanism—like the classical analysis before it—was based on the

---

[7] These terms are not exact equivalents and there is a small literature on distinctions between *monopolistic* and *imperfect* competition. Our main interest in this section will be to see how these new theories recognized important monopoly elements even in apparently competitive situations, and, hence, the term *monopolistic competition* is perhaps slightly preferable for our uses.

[8] This does not exhaust the list of authors working in this field in the late 'twenties and early 'thirties. We should add at least two others: the versatile British economist R. F. Harrod, and the German theorist Heinrich von Stackelberg.

assumption of large numbers of small firms none of which is big enough to have any influence over the market for its product. Along with this had grown up a separate theory of monopolized industries—that is, industries in which one large firm controls the entire supply of a particular product. Thus, there were really two cases which economists could analyze: (1) the case of pure competition, on which the whole of general equilibrium theory was based; and (2) the case of pure monopoly, which, hopefully, mopped up the exceptions to pure competition which might be found in practice.

Now the difficulty for anyone looking at the real world in the 1920's—or before or since, for that matter—was to find examples that fit *either* case. In the case of monopoly, a few instances might perhaps be cited in the public utilities field, but as far as most of industry was concerned even the very largest firms typically had at least *some* competitors. Take the American automobile industry in the late 1920's. Ford was the leading car producer during most of this period, but it definitely had its rivals. Indeed, by 1931, General Motors had gone permanently into the lead with some 43 per cent of the market. The Chrysler Corporation had been formed in 1925, and it, too, was a strong competitor, taking second place from Ford in 1937. There was definitely a "Big Three" in the automobile industry, but hardly a single-firm monopoly. Other industries showed different particular patterns but the general principle was the same. U.S. Steel was a very large firm in the 1920's with some 35 to 40 per cent of the industry's ingot capacity, but its share of the market was actually declining over time and it also had numerous rivals in Bethlehem, Republic, Jones and Laughlin, Youngstown, and many other smaller firms who, together, held a quite considerable share of the market. It was clear to anyone who searched that cases of pure monopoly—a single seller controlling the *entire* supply of a product—were extremely rare.

But the situation was really no better when it came to the matter of pure competition. Where were all the sellers who were so small and powerless that they had *no effect whatever* on the prices of their products—i.e., were completely at the mercy of impersonal market forces? The corner grocery store might seem about as small an economic venture as it was possible to undertake, and there were countless thousands of them in existence in the 1920's. But did not even this minuscule economic undertaking have just a little bit of control over its prices? Was it not the case, observed daily by every housewife in the country, that some grocery stores charged a little more and others a little less for this or that product? Indeed, wasn't the problem quite universal? Whenever and wherever a housewife went shopping, she found not identical products each going at the same price but rather similar—not quite the same—products going at slightly different—not quite the same—prices. In 1929, Ivory soap was a big seller with its heavily advertised claim of special purity. If the makers of Ivory had decided to raise its price by a penny, or even by a nickel, undoubtedly some purists would have continued **77** to buy. Would this have meant that the makers of Ivory were in a monopoly position? Evidently they were not pure competitors because they would have shown at least *some* control over the price of their product. Except possibly for certain agricultural markets, pure competition was proving to be every bit as elusive as pure monopoly.

This was obviously an unsatisfactory state of affairs, and what this group of economists in the 1920's and early 1930's attempted to find was a way of "blending" the separate theories of monopoly and competition into a more general theory of value. In this more general theory, pure competition and pure monopoly would, ideally, appear simply as special limiting cases.

In the end, as it turned out, this general problem proved somewhat refractory to theoretical analysis and it remains without a complete solution even today. Nevertheless, certain definite forward steps were made in this period and they were of a specific and systematic kind. One of these steps had to do with what was called *product differentiation,* a subject that looms particularly large in Professor Chamberlin's treatment:

> One way of "blending" monopolistic and competitive elements along a spectrum is by considering the degree of difference between the products various firms produce. "Monopoly" occurs when a firm controls the supply of a particular product. "Competition" occurs when there are very large numbers of firms producing an identical product. Now if we look at a real situation—say, the retail market for soap products—we find both elements present. There are large numbers of sellers of a roughly similar product, "soap," and hence there is a form of competition involved. But, at the same time, each particular producer has an absolute monopoly on his special brand of soap: Ivory, Lifebuoy, Lux, Palmolive, etc. Each producer thus: (1) has some control over the price of his particular product, and (2) is subject to competition from products only slightly "differentiated" from his. We could now, if we wished, construct a series of cases that moved imperceptibly from pure competition on the one hand to pure monopoly on the other. At the competitive end, we have large numbers of firms producing exactly the same product. Then we move to the case where there is a little product differentiation—e.g., brand-names. Then we move along to the case where the substitutes are substantially different products and, finally, completing the spectrum, to the case of pure monopoly where there are no substitutes at all.[9]

This view of the problem was not only insightful and more realistic than what had gone before but it also led to certain analytic consequences. For one thing, as Chamberlin was at some pains to show, the prices charged and quantities produced by firms operating in this form of monopolistic competition were in general different from what they would be under pure competition. Under certain assumptions, for example, it could be demonstrated that the

[9] A moment's reflection will convince anyone that *pure* monopoly in this view— i.e., no substitutes at all—is a very rare phenomenon. Indeed, since all products—food, clothing, washing-machines—are to some extent substitutes for one another, pure monopoly would occur only when there is, in Chamberlin's words, "control of the supply of all economic goods by the same person or agency—" i.e., monopoly of the total economy!

price would be higher and the quantity produced lower by a monopolistically competitive than by a purely competitive firm. Indeed, if purely competitive output were taken as a norm, monopolistically competitive firms would often be found to be operating with "excess capacity." [10]

Equally important, however, was that it greatly broadened economists' views about the functions of a business firm. Under pure competition, the individual firm had little to do but keep down its costs and produce the output which would be most profitable at given market prices. With monopolistic elements intervening, however, it now became clear that the typical business firm had many other areas of discretion and decision. Price was not a given but a variable, to some degree under the firm's control. So was the product. A businessman might choose to compete with his rivals not by altering price but by making changes—trivial or substantial—in his particular product, which would differentiate it from other products in the minds of consumers. Finally, and not least important, the whole phenomenon of advertising could now for the first time be brought into systematic economic analysis. Economists had, of course, long recognized the *factual* importance of advertising, but the truth was that this phenomenon had had no place at all in the main structure of economic *theory*. For the purely competitive firm does not advertise. Advertising implies a "differentiated" product or at least some control over the general market for a commodity. And these conditions are incompatible with the assumptions of pure competition. Advertising is characteristically *both* "monopolistic" *and* "competitive," and, by giving it a proper home, these new theories clearly brought a much higher degree of realism to the analysis of business behavior.

As we have said, this new approach met a direct and enthusiastic response among economists, and there were even some who imagined that another "revolution" in economics was occurring. And, in a way, it was; although, with the advantage of hindsight, one is impressed not only by what was achieved but also by what was not achieved. For the truth is that the new theories of monopolistic competition did not drive the old theory of pure competition from the field as one might have expected. The latter is still going strong in many areas of economic theory and, indeed, the impact of the analysis of monopolistic competition has been felt most strongly in the applied fields of industrial organization.

The main explanation for this is that while the new analysis was properly systematic, it produced satisfactory results only for *part* of the problem under consideration, and, in some respects, not the most important part. For it is characteristic of modern industrial firms not only that they differentiate their

---

[10] The central reason why a firm in monopolistic competition would typically produce less than one in pure competition is that the former must take into account the *fall* in price that will occur with each expansion of output. In pure competition the price is taken by each firm as given by the market.

products but also that they are *big*. They are big in the sense that in many important industries a relatively small number of firms largely dominate the national market for the given product. To put this another way, one can range firms and industries along the monopoly-competition spectrum not only by degrees of product differentiation but also in terms of the numbers of firms in the industry. One firm is "monopoly," two firms give "duopoly," several firms "oligopoly" and so on until, with many, many firms, we reach "competition." What we are saying is that, in many modern industrial situations, the organization is typically some form of "oligopoly."

Now the theorists of the 1920's and 1930's were not insensitive to this problem of size and numbers. Indeed, economists had struggled with it before. As early as 1838, Augustin Cournot, whose efforts in mathematical economics we have mentioned, had developed an approach to the problem of "duopoly." Later in the century, Pareto worked on the problem, as did the English economist Francis Y. Edgeworth. The new theorists of monopolistic competition were aware of this work, extended it, and some of them, such as Heinrich von Stackelberg, made elaborate efforts to cope with the oligopoly problem. Their achievement in this respect, however, was only a limited one. The central difficulty with analyzing industries in which there are a few large firms is that these firms are necessarily aware that their own actions affect the positions of other firms in the industry and that these other firms are also aware of this fact. The pattern of actions and reactions which can occur under these circumstances is enormously complex and, although the theorists of the early 1930's made the problem explicit, they found no general and systematic solution for it.

The consequence has been that subsequent work on the oligopoly problem has gone forward on rather different lines from those indicated by the monopolistic competition theorists. Some of it has been of a highly empirical nature involving specific "industry studies" in which the characteristic behavioral patterns of particular industries are set forth in great factual detail. Some of it has been extremely theoretical and mathematical.

A good example of the latter is the use of what is known as *game theory* to help economists understand the complicated patterns of action and reaction typical of oligopolistic markets. This particular effort stems largely from the work of the mathematician John von Neumann (1903-1957), and the economist Oskar Morgenstern (b. 1902), whose classic work, *Theory of Games and Economic Behavior,* was published in 1944. The analogy of a game to a business situation in which each firm must base its actions on what it expects other firms to do can easily be seen. Consider, for example, the following game. The dollar sums in the table below are the amounts Player *B* must pay to Player *A* depending upon the outcome of the game. The rules of the game are that Player *B* can choose any column he wishes and that Player *A* can choose any row. Player *A* wants to receive as large a payment as possible; Player *B* wants to make as small a payment as possible. Which row should *A* choose and which column should *B* choose?

| Player A | Player B can choose the column | | |
can	A	B	C
choose (1)	$10	$3	$0
the row. (2)	0	3	7
(3)	6	5	6

In this simple game, B must pay A the dollar amounts shown depending on the final position achieved. An *equilibrium* position is achieved at Row 3, Column B ($5 payment).

It is clear that what is best for *A* to do will depend on what *B* does, and vice versa. And this is exactly analogous to a business situation where one firm's decision on price, or advertising policy, or product design will depend on another firm's similar decision and both firms are aware of this fact.

One way of approaching this particular game is to say that *A* will try to maximize the minimum payment he can get from *B*. By this logic, he would choose Row 3, since in that row, no matter what *B* does, he will get at least $5 (in either of the other two rows he might possibly get nothing!). By contrast, *B* may try to minimize the maximum payment he will have to make to *A*. He would choose Column B since there the maximum he must pay *A* is $5 (in the other two columns it would be $10 and $7). Indeed, in game theory terminology, this position—Row 3, Column *B*—is described as an *equilibrium* position, since neither party will have reason to change his strategy if the other does not change.[11]

Despite the development of game and decision theory in recent years, however, the oligopoly problem still remains with us and this helps explain why the "unrealistic" and essentially late-nineteenth century theory of pure competition continues to play an important role in present-day economics. Competitive theory remains the only truly systematic general theory of value and distribution which economists possess. If they wish to develop systematic theories of other subjects—growth, for example, or depressions and unemployment—they have little practical recourse than to base themselves in the admittedly over-simplified competitive world.[12]

[11] The strategies of *A* and *B* in this example are called, respectively, *minimax* and *maximin* strategies. For a full discussion of game theory in clear but still rather technical terms see R. Duncan Luce and Howard Raiffa, *Games and Decisions* (New York: Wiley, 1957).

For a discussion of various other modern approaches to the oligopoly problem, see, in this Series, Richard Caves, *American Industry: Structure, Conduct, Performance*, 2nd ed., especially Chapters 2 and 3.

[12] Another important reason for the survival of the "unrealistic" theory of pure competition is that it is useful in welfare economics, as providing a standard of economic "efficiency." This refers to the "ideal" properties of the purely competitive solution referred to in the last chapter (p. 62). Other market forms can then be compared and contrasted with the competitive norm.

This is not to say that the theories of monopolistic competition had no lasting impact. They did. Not only did they point up explicitly the limitations of the traditional analysis—limitations which economists have never since been free to lose sight of—but they opened new avenues of research into the ways in which modern industrial firms actually do behave. In this sense, this third departure from traditional theory has something in common with the writings of Veblen and Schumpeter discussed earlier. In all three cases, the effort had as a central purpose to call economists' attention to discrepancies between their theoretical models and the awkward but pungent realities of the world about them. In none of the cases were the discrepancies completely removed. But in each case the summons to research—research about what the modern industrial world really involves—was clear and insistent.

SUMMARY

In this chapter, we have taken up three attempts from the early decades of this century to modify, and make more realistic, traditional economic theory.

The most dramatic criticisms of traditional theory came from Thorstein Veblen who wanted a richer, sociologically more penetrating, and more definitely evolutionary economics than mainstream analysis provided. His influence on the evolution of modern economics was more indirect than direct, but he did leave behind some important concepts (e.g., "conspicuous consumption"), some quasi-followers (the institutionalist school), and above all, a refreshingly skeptical outlook on the grave achievements of pure economic theory.

Schumpeter sought not to overthrow traditional theory but to use it as a point of departure for a different problem: the problem of economic growth. His emphasis on entrepreneurship and innovation was important and he showed how, by taking long-range growth considerations into account, one's views on all basic economic problems might be altered. Schumpeter's influence in the 1930's was less than it might have been because, among other things, of the short-run problem of acute depression, but his influence has been growing as economists of the present-day show more and more interest in the field of economic development.

The third attempt to modify late-nineteenth century analysis was the most closely related to traditional thinking. An outgrowth of the natural technical evolution of the subject, the theories of imperfect and monopolistic competition were the product of several minds (Sraffa, Chamberlin, Robinson, von Stackelberg, etc.) and were clearly an improvement in the sense of bring-

ing greater realism to this area of economic theory. That they did not have as revolutionary an impact as might have been expected was due partly to the difficulty of the problem, especially the oligopoly problem. (Modern game theory is a significant effort to cope with this theoretically complex problem.) It was also due to the continuing value of the theory of pure competition because of its systematic and normative characteristics. The net impact of *all* these developments, however, was quite considerable, and its direction was clearly that of bringing economic theory closer to the realities of economic life.

The Keynesian Revolution

The most dramatic change in modern economics in the twentieth century, however, came from another direction. It was like these earlier departures in that it called for a closer correspondence between economic theory and economic reality, but it differed from them in subject matter, approach, and in its extraordinary impact. It was the product of a long evolution within mainstream economics and it was deeply conditioned by the course of actual economic events. Still, the whole thing crystallized in a particular year with the publication of a particular book by a particular man. The year was 1936. The book was *The General Theory of Employment, Interest and Money*. And the man was John Maynard Keynes, later Lord Keynes, Baron of Tilton.

HERESIES AND HARD TIMES

To understand the real implications of this development —and to put in perspective a matter which many to this day still regard as controversial—it is necessary to retrace our steps and consider certain aspects of earlier economic thought that have so far been mentioned only in a passing way.

The central economic question at issue and the problem to which Keynes ultimately addressed himself was this: What forces determine the levels of output and employment, not so much in particular industries, but in an economy *as a whole?* We now ask:

85

How did earlier economists attack this question of the determination of total (or *aggregate*) employment and output? Did they recognize the problem? If they did, what answers did they offer?

Recognition of the problem—at least in the sense of observing that nations sometimes experience times when business is slow and jobs hard to find or, conversely, when there is general prosperity—dates back to the beginnings of modern economics. The problem could not have arisen much earlier because it is characteristic of a modern, commercial, market economy, and would have a very different form in a decentralized, agrarian world. With the great commercial expansion of the sixteenth century, however, writers on economic matters began to take note and several mercantilist pamphleteers expressed concern about the employment problem. The concern was manifested in a "fear of goods"—i.e., a fear that the importation of foreign commodities might displace domestic industries and jobs. It was related to the characteristic mercantilist views about a favorable balance of trade and securing foreign treasure that we have already discussed.[1]

With the triumph of classical economics in the late-eighteenth and early-nineteenth centuries, however, the problem receded into the background. This was not a matter of inattention; rather, the classical economists had definite theoretical reasons for believing that departures from full employment in the economy as a whole would be temporary and rare. These reasons—whether ultimately right or wrong—were based on a more sophisticated analysis than the mercantilists had offered and involved essentially two points. First, there was a separation of the problem of money from the analysis of the real economy beneath the monetary veil, often through the use of the quantity theory of money. This point we have taken up before. Second, the underlying real economy was believed to be subject to what was called *Say's law,* after Jean Baptiste Say, the French economist already known to us for his work on utility theory. This law stated that, for the economy as a whole, "supply creates its own demand"; that is, that there can be no such thing as a deficiency of "aggregate demand." There can be overproduction of *particular* commodities, but not overproduction in *general*. The reasoning behind this law is not difficult to understand. Once we banish money from our economy, it is clear that the way in which we "demand" one set of commodities is simply by offering other commodities for them. Whenever we produce an additional "supply" of commodities, therefore, we are adding to the "demand" for commodities at the same time. We produce, say, an additional 10 pairs of shoes. Either we want these for our own use (in which case there is no problem of "demand" to worry us) or we offer them in exchange for other commodities (bread, safety-pins, etc.). In the latter case we are increasing "demand" for these other products through our increased "supply" of shoes. It is true that other producers may not want additional shoes at the going prices. In this case, the price of shoes in terms of other commodities (bread,

[1] For the discussion of mercantilist views, see pp. 4-5.

safety-pins) may fall. But this is nothing but to say that the relative prices of these other commodities have *risen*. Being intelligent profit-seeking producers, we shall next year produce not more shoes but more bread and safety-pins! The combination of Say's law and the separation of real from monetary economics thus makes a deficiency of aggregate demand seem a virtual impossibility.

This approach did not command universal assent at the time. Malthus, in particular, worried about the problem and engaged in a fascinating correspondence with Ricardo in which he endeavored to show that a "universal glut" of commodities could take place if capitalists and landowners became too frugal in their saving habits.[2] Ricardo was a firm believer in Say's law, but even he came to think that unemployment might take place in one special case: when machinery was introduced to replace labor. This possibility of technological unemployment was dramatically developed by Marx in his theory of the Industrial Reserve Army (above, pp. 37-38). Still, these were exceptions to the rule, and this remained the case through most of the nineteenth century. The objectors, like Marx, tended to be heretics in other ways as well, men who wished to throw out not only Say's law but most of traditional economic theory.

Toward the end of the nineteenth century, however, this state of affairs began to change appreciably. Business fluctuations and their causes were attracting more and more attention from economists. Jevons offered the theory that periodic commercial cycles were connected with good and bad harvests, these in turn being influenced by meteorological conditions. Marshall took up the problem of commercial crises in his *Economics of Industry* (written in 1879, jointly with his wife) and also contributed, as did other leading economists, to the development of a more sophisticated theory of the role of money in the economy. Marshall was Keynes' teacher and his influence on his pupil has often been noted.[3]

But the most striking forward step at this time was that taken by the great Swedish economist, Knut Wicksell (1851-1926), whose classic work, *Interest and Prices,* appeared in Sweden in 1898. Wicksell concerned himself directly with a number of problems that were to prove crucial in what followed.

---

[2] Malthus' concern involved the possibility that if all capitalists and landowners turned away from consumption to saving and capital accumulation, they would at the same time: (a) greatly expand the production of goods to be consumed (more capital has been applied to productive purposes) and (b) provide an inadequate market for consuming these goods (since, by hypothesis, all capitalists and landlords are turning away from consumption to saving). Hence a "universal glut" would result. In reality, Malthus' argument was far from air-tight and the logically-minded Ricardo had little difficulty disposing of it. The controversy—which can be followed in detail in the *Works of Ricardo* (ed. P. Sraffa)—provides a fascinating example of the never-ending problem in economics: the conflict between theoretical virtue (Ricardo) and cloudy realism (Malthus).

[3] See, for example, Harry G. Johnson, "How Important Is Cambridge to Keynesian Economics?", reprinted in Robert Lekachman, *Keynes and the Classics* (Boston: Heath, 1964).

In particular, he distinguished between a *natural* rate of interest, determined by basic technological factors, and a *money* rate of interest, the rate actually charged in the money market at a particular moment in time. When the natural rate was above the money rate, businessmen generally would be able to make greater profits by increasing their capital investments, and this would lead to an expansionary phase in the economy as a whole. When the natural rate was below the money rate (i.e., when it cost more to borrow than basic technological factors warranted), then the demand for new capital might be "practically nil" and there would be "bad times" all around.

Wicksell's analysis was incomplete but it was significant for many reasons. For one thing, there was the apparent effort to link together the real and monetary sides of the economic system. The economy expands or contracts when the real factors, operating on the natural rate of interest, diverge from the monetary factors, operating on the money rate of interest. For another thing, the emphasis is on the economy as a whole rather than on the inter-relationships of its component parts. Wicksell was trying to apply the notion of supply and demand, customarily used for determining the prices of particular commodities, to the general price level. He was thus necessarily raising questions about aggregate demand and supply that differentiate him from a follower of Say's law. Finally, and not least important, he focused on the important problem of saving and investment decisions. During the boom phase, when investment is high, Wicksell was aware that savings might not keep pace. He was aware, in other words, that saving and investment decisions were not the same decisions and that discrepancies between them might have important effects on the economy as a whole. This point, as we shall see in a moment, was a vital one in the new analysis.

By the end of the nineteenth century, then, an important beginning had been made; and by the early decades of the twentieth century, the whole subject of business cycles was very much in the air. The concluding chapter of Schumpeter's *Theory of Economic Development* (1911) was devoted to it. Wesley Mitchell's *Business Cycles* was first published in 1913. In Sweden, meanwhile, Wicksell's followers were active and, in the 'twenties and early 'thirties, the so-called "Stockholm School"—Professors Lindahl, Myrdal, Ohlin, and others—was directing much of its attention to aggregative problems and to the question of unemployment in particular.

Simultaneously, actual economic conditions were demanding a more adequate explanation than traditional theory could offer. There had always been evidence of an unemployment problem in the industrial countries. In Britain, for example, the percentage of unemployed among the unionized labor force from 1860 to World War I had regularly fluctuated from 1-2 per cent to 8-10 per cent. World War I was followed by a short but very sharp industrial contraction in Europe and the United States. The 1920's were buoyant for the most part, but then in 1929 came the great "crash" on Wall Street and the beginning of perhaps the worst depression in history. In the

United States, for example, unemployment, which stood at a little over 3 per cent of the labor force in 1929, had risen to 16 per cent in 1931 and to 25 per cent—a quarter of the labor-force!—by 1933. Total American production (Gross National Product) in that year was down even more, perhaps two-thirds of what it had been in 1929. Nor was this a short-lived phenomenon. In 1941—the year the United States entered World War II—10 per cent of the labor force still was out of work. The Great Depression was international in its effects, and it is no coincidence that the year 1933 was also the year that Adolph Hitler took power in Germany.

By the early 'thirties the gap between traditional views and glaring economic realities had become dramatically evident. The phenomenon was too vast to be accounted for in terms of exceptions or patchwork corrections. It needed to be dealt with *within* the central body of economic theory, a goal which would obviously require a substantial reconstruction of what had long been accepted. And it was to this task of general reconstruction that Keynes addressed himself.

THE KEYNESIAN THEORY

Reasonable men differ about the ultimate verdict history will pronounce on his theories, but that Keynes was a man of exceptional brilliance and easily the most influential economist of the past thirty or forty years no informed person can doubt.

The Man

John Maynard Keynes (1883-1946) was born into the very same intellectual world in which he was later to secure his most lasting achievements. His childhood was spent in the shadow of Cambridge University where his father, John Neville Keynes, was an eminent logician and political economist. The father's achievements, particularly his *Scope and Method of Political Economy* (1891), have distinction in their own right, though they were presently overshadowed by the more formidable performances of the son.

Keynes' range of activities was extraordinary. He was, at various times in his life, a high government official, an editor, a publisher, a businessman, a teacher, a college administrator, a member of a distinguished literary set, a patron of the arts, a book-collector, and, of course, the foremost economist of his age. Most of these things he did simultaneously and in each case with what would normally be considered outstanding success. Lying in his bed each morning before arising, he took care of his business and financial speculations, producing in this way a fortune which was estimated at his death to be around £450,000, or somewhat under $2 million. As Bursar of King's College, Cambridge, he not only completely reconstructed the College's financial affairs but took an active role in all aspects of college life. His interest in literature

89

and the arts brought him into the famous "Bloomsbury" set, which included such gifted talents as Virginia Woolf, Leonard Woolf, Lytton Strachey, Duncan Grant, E. M. Forster, and many others. His wife, the former Lydia Lopokova, was a prima ballerina, and presently Keynes was involved in the world of the theater. In 1936, the year he published his *General Theory,* The Arts Theatre in Cambridge was opened, a project for which Keynes bore responsibility from start to finish.[4]

His versatility also showed in his writings. His first major intellectual effort was his *Treatise on Probability* (published in 1921, though mainly completed much earlier), a serious attack on the root problems of inductive knowledge. Even his economic writings varied widely in tone and purpose. Some, like his *Economic Consequences of the Peace,* were addressed to immediate current problems, were written at white heat, and produced widespread public reaction. The *General Theory,* by contrast, was intended to deal with fundamentals, was the product of a long evolution in his thinking, and, as its very first sentence announces, was "chiefly addressed to my fellow economists."

His thoughts about economic matters developed considerably over time and, for this reason, it is possible to find inconsistencies in his writings. Keynes, like Emerson, did not care much for consistency for its own sake. On closer inspection, however, it is clear that there was a very definite continuity between his earlier and his mature outlook on economic problems. More than a decade before the *General Theory* was published, Keynes was already advocating most of the public measures that were later to become associated with his name. What he lacked then—and what he set about to develop—was the analysis that would give substance to his intuition.

The Nature of the Departure

Keynes wrote in the preface to the *General Theory* that future critics "will fluctuate, I expect, between a belief that I am quite wrong and a belief that I am saying nothing new." As a prediction, this very much understated the impact the book was to have, but it does suggest, as is in fact the case, that there are strong continuities between Keynesian thought and the traditional theory it was meant to replace.

To mention a few examples: Keynes accepted the traditional assumption of a purely competitive economy. The great outburst of interest in monopolistic and oligopolistic competition has no echo in the *General Theory*—speaking always of the basic analytic structure, not of the various and often insightful side-comments he made along the way. Keynes also accepted many of the behavioral assumptions of standard theory. Producers, in the Keynesian

---

[4] For an interesting account of the many aspects of Keynes' life and their influence on his work in economics, see R. F. Harrod, *The Life of John Maynard Keynes* (New York: Harcourt, Brace, 1951). Harrod is a distinguished economist whose contributions we have mentioned above (p. 76) and will come to again (pp. 98-99).

world, engage in simple profit-maximization just as they did in the world of Walras or Ricardo. Marginal analysis is used extensively throughout. Furthermore, Keynes presented his theory in the essentially static form characteristic of the late-nineteenth century analysis. There is no growth in the Keynesian system, nor any formal analysis of processes of change. Fundamental conditions—technology, population, stock of capital—are taken as given.

Also, and perhaps somewhat surprisingly, Keynes took a rather traditional view of the institutional setting of economic life. That is to say, he took that setting, including the nature of the State, as given independently of the existing economic situation. Of course, as everyone knows, Keynes did urge a different and larger role for the State than had many of his predecessors. But he had no theory as to how economic factors would bring about changes in the structure of the State. Like most mainstream economists before him (and after him, as well), he took the basic institutions of his time and country as given without need for explanation.

So much for continuities. What of contrasts? What caused economists after the *General Theory* to speak of the "new economics"? What caused Keynes himself to write George Bernard Shaw that he believed his work "will largely revolutionize—not, I suppose, at once but in the course of the next ten years—the way the world thinks about economic problems"?

Let us characterize the Keynesian departures in a general way and then, in the next section, briefly give the analysis by which they were justified. The following five points are interrelated but each deserves separate mention:

1. Keynesian economics deals primarily with large economic aggregates—national output, total employment, the general price level—rather than particular firms, industries, households, and their various interrelationships.

The distinction here is between what economists call *macro-economics* as opposed to *micro-economics*. Keynes did not invent *macro-economics*—large parts of classical economics were macro-economic in nature, so also were the pre-Keynesian business cycle theories we have just mentioned—but he gave an enormous stimulus to this particular approach. Traditional general equilibrium theory was unequivocally micro-economic in its basic structure; Keynes put the focus on grand social "totals" and the generalizations that could be derived from them.

2. Keynesian economics gives great weight to the concept of "aggregate demand." The basic components of aggregate demand are total consumer demand, total business investment demand, and total government demand. A fundamental question in Keynesian economics is whether aggregate demand and aggregate supply are in a proper balance.

Keynes emphasized a question that ran directly counter to the contentions embodied in Say's law. He asked: Will the total of all demands— consumption, investment, and government—for the goods and services of the economy be sufficient to purchase all the goods and services the economy is capable of supplying when it is operating at the full employment level?

> 3. In Keynesian economics, full employment (and the level of total output corresponding to that level of employment) is treated as a special case. Full employment happens only when aggregate demand and aggregate supply are equal at the full employment level. But this may not happen. The economy may be in equilibrium with inflationary conditions or— and this was the point stressed—with substantial mass unemployment.

Keynesian economics has sometimes been described as the economics of "underemployment equilibrium." This is not a fully accurate description but it does point up the fact that Keynes emphasized the possibility that unemployment might be a phenomenon not of *disequilibrium* in the economy but of *equilibrium.* Traditional theory, on the whole, argued that if unemployment existed, a reduction in the worker's wages would induce employers to hire more workers and thus cure the problem. Keynes pointed out that such a cut in wages could be guaranteed to bring an expansion in employment only if the demand for the employers' products remained the same. But with *all* wages being cut this would bring a fall in the money incomes of the wage earners and hence a general fall in the demand for business' products. Thus, the wage-cut might have little if any direct effect on the central problem. Indeed, Keynes asserted that there might be *no* way in which ordinary market forces could correct the unemployment situation.[5]

> 4. Keynesian economics placed great importance upon the integration of the theories of monetary phenomena and real phenomena and, in particular, showed the role of "money" in determining the levels of such real variables as total output and employment.

In one of the last chapters of the *General Theory,* Keynes resurrected the mercantilists, Malthus, and a number of nineteenth-century heretics who had, as he argued, perceived intuitively that money was not simply a veil but an important variable in the nation's economic well-being. Keynes argued that people had various different motives for wanting to hold money, that it was not simply a colorless "medium of exchange," and that the quantity theory of money—again, except in certain special cases—was false. With the development of a more elaborate monetary theory, he was able to attack Say's law at its foundations.

> 5. As a consequence of the foregoing, Keynesian economics found the feasible remedies for unemployment and below capacity output not in

[5] There was a heated, and not very fruitful, controversy in the years following the publication of the *General Theory* as to whether there really was unemployment *equilibrium* in the Keynesian system, since, presumably, money wages would be falling. This led some commentators to claim that unemployment in the Keynesian world depended on the existence of *rigid wages.* The central point Keynes was making, however, was not that wages were rigid (though he thought they often were) but that, even if they were flexible downward, wage-cuts in general would fail to correct an unemployment situation.

the automatic workings of the market but in a more active intervention by the State. This intervention would typically consist in measures to affect the nation's "aggregate demand" either directly—by government taxes and expenditures—or, more indirectly—by actions influencing the supply of money.

This fifth point is what many people have in mind when they think of "Keynesian economics." Since an evaluation of this matter necessarily involves some understanding of the analysis behind it, however, we shall defer it momentarily, turning first to the theory itself.

Essentials of the Theory

Underlying the general approach we have just described were several insights into the workings of a modern economy. None of these insights was completely original with Keynes, but their incorporation into a systematic theory of the total economic process represented originality of the highest order.

We can approach this systematic theory by means of two questions: (1) How can it be that aggregate demand can fall short at the full employment level with a given rate of interest? (2) Why does not the interest rate change in such a way as to insure us full employment? In other words, we are going at the basic question in stages, first taking the interest rate as given, then asking what happens when we allow the interest rate to become a variable.

To answer *Question 1* along Keynesian lines, we must ask, first, what factors determine the various components of aggregate demand—consumption demand, investment demand and government demand? Since we are, for the moment, investigating the possibilities of unemployment in a market economy, we shall assume that government demand is either small or non-existent. The main components of private demand are the consumption demands of households and the investment demands of businesses for additional plant, equipment, machinery, inventories, and so one. What determines the size of these demands?

As far as consumption is concerned, Keynes argued that the main factor determining an individual's (or society's) level of consumption would be the individual's (or society's) level of income. In particular, Keynes brought forth what he called a "fundamental psychological law." According to this law, when a person's income rises he will in general divide the increase between added consumption and added saving. For society as a whole, Keynes concluded, an increase in national income (the total production of the nation) will lead to an increase both in the amount people wish to consume in total and the amount they wish to save in total.

As far as business investment demand is concerned, Keynes pointed out that these decisions were affected by many different factors, including the general expectations of future business conditions and also the cost of borrowing funds—i.e., the interest rate. Since we are dealing with *Question 1,*

93

we may momentarily consider the interest rate as given. This means that changes in the level of business investment demand will depend on changes in the general expectations businessmen have about the profitability of adding to their plant, machinery, and other equipment.

Now notice that we are already in a position to give an answer to our preliminary *Question 1*. In our private economy the total demand for goods and services will be equal to the sum of consumption demand and business investment demand. Let us suppose that the income the society is capable of producing at full employment is $100 billion of goods and services. Let us suppose, further, that at this level of national income, consumers wish to consume $85 billion and to save the rest, or $15 billion. (Savings in the Keynesian system are defined as that part of income which is not consumed.) Let us suppose, finally, that, at the given interest rate and with business expectations as they happen to be, business investment demand is $10 billion. Under these circumstances, can the economy stay at the full employment level?

Keynes' answer would be: *no*. The reason is that at the full employment level there will be $100 billion worth of goods produced by the society but there will not be sufficient aggregate demand for them. In particular, aggregate demand will equal the sum of consumption demand ($85 billion) and investment demand ($10 billion) or, in total, $95 billion. Aggregate supply exceeds aggregate demand by $5 billion. And what happens now is that businessmen, seeing that they are unable to sell all they are producing, begin to cut back on production and employment. National income falls. Will this fall in national income help bring about an equilibrium? Keynes' answer to this question would be: *yes*. For, with the fall in national income, consumption will fall but not by as much as income. Or, equivalently, savings will fall as national income falls. We may imagine that a lower level of income is reached wherein the new level of consumption demand plus the $10 billion dollar investment demand is now equal to national income. This will occur, in our example, when savings and investment are equal. An equilibrium situation might be as follows:

National Income $(Y) = \$80$ billion
Business Investment Demand $(I) = \$10$ billion
Consumption demand $(C) = \$70$ billion

Here, aggregate demand $(C+I)$ equals national income (Y), at the level of $80 billion. At this point, savings (S) equal investment at $10 billion. Remember that this is an equilibrium situation but *not* a full employment situation. Indeed, a society capable of producing $100 billion worth of output is, in our example, producing only $80 billion. Such a situation would normally mean a great deal of unemployment.[6]

What is happening here, in essence, is that national income is adjusting downward to correct a disequilibrium between aggregate demand and supply. The

---

[6] The reader should notice that in our simplifield model the statements (1) that consumption demand plus investment demand equals national income and (2) that investment demand equals savings are equivalent. This is because savings (S) are here defined as: $S = Y - C$. When $C + I = Y$, then, $S = I$ necessarily follows.

problem arises because consumption plus investment demand is too small, or equivalently, the desire of households to save exceeds the desire of businesses to invest. If, as much traditional theory had maintained, decisions to save and decisions to invest were essentially the same decision, there could be no problem. But Keynes (like Wicksell) perceived that savings decisions and investment decisions were not the same. They were characteristically made by different people and influenced by different factors. Thus, it might happen that savings decisions exceeded investment decisions, and when this did happen, Keynes argued, aggregate demand would be insufficient to sustain the going rate of national income. The result: a fall in income and general unemployment!

But this is only one part of the picture. And, indeed, a moment's reflection will convince anyone that the analysis so far presented contains a potentially serious flaw. For if the problem can be thought of as too much saving (or too little consumption demand) relative to investment, then may not the whole difficulty disappear when we allow the interest rate to change? The possibility seems very reasonable. We are faced with a situation in which there are a great many savers and too few investors. Won't these savers simply offer to lend for less? Won't this fall in the interest rate encourage more investment? In short, will there not be forces generated to bring down the interest rate so that saving and investment decisions can be equated *at* the full employment level?

This, of course, takes us directly to *Question 2*. In particular, we now have to ask of Keynes: why does not the rate of interest fall to a level low enough to equate savings and investment decisions *without* a fall in employment and national income? [7] And this question leads to another important area of Keynesian theory. Indeed, it is here that money makes its fateful entrance upon the scene.

For, in the Keynesian world, the fundamental reason why the rate of interest does not go indefinitely downward is that, after a certain point, people would sooner hold their assets in the form of money, and this creates a floor beneath which the interest rate cannot fall. When the interest rate is low enough, the savers who have the funds will no longer offer to lend them to business investors at still lower rates; instead, they will simply hold their wealth in the form of money. When this point is reached, the forces that might be expected to bring the interest rate down further lose effect. And yet there still may be too little investment and hence general unemployment in the economy.

Needless to say, all this presupposes that there is something rather special about money, and Keynes found this special quality in the attribute

---

[7] Of course it might be that business expectations were so grim that no matter how low the interest rate was, investment would still fall short of full employment savings. In this important case there would be unemployment even at a zero rate of interest.

he called *liquidity*. *Liquidity* means, in Keynes' words, "immediate command over goods in general." Since money is the universally accepted medium of exchange, it is clearly perfectly *liquid* in this sense. A typical individual is faced with the decision not only as to how much of his income he wishes to save as opposed to consume but also how much of his wealth he wishes to hold in the form of perfectly liquid money as opposed to relatively less liquid assets such as stocks and bonds.

Keynes then said that there were various motives leading individuals to desire liquidity. Some of these—such as the desire to be able to carry out day-to-day purchases and the desire to have certain funds ready for unforeseen contingencies—were obvious and quite in accord with standard views about the role of money. But he then stressed a further motive—what he called the "speculative motive"—which was likely to be greatly influenced by the rate of interest. When the interest rate is low, market speculators will develop a strong *liquidity preference*. Since the reward they get for holding less liquid assets is low, why not hold money instead? And if interest rates are low, there is a greater likelihood that the prices of stocks and bonds will fall, thus causing losses which may far outweigh the gains from earning interest.[8]

Thus, the lower the interest rate, the greater will be the desire to hold wealth in the form of money. If there is a limited supply of money in the economy, the interest rate which equilibrates the desire to hold money with the amount available may actually be quite high, meaning low investment and high unemployment. Even if there is a large supply of money in the economy, the interest rate will not go down indefinitely because at very low rates people may wish to hold all their extra wealth in the form of money and no one will be offering to buy stocks and bonds at higher prices (i.e., lower interest rates). In this case too, general unemployment is possible.

With our second question now answered, it is possible to summarize the central drift of Keynes' *General Theory* in the following capsule form:

> The equilibrium level of national income and the equilibrium rate of interest will be determined simultaneously in such fashion that (1) the amount consumers want to save and the amount businessmen want to invest are equal; and (2) the amount of their wealth people wish to hold in the form of money and the actual amount of money available in the economy are equal. This equilibrium situation is not necessarily a full employment situation. Indeed, if consumers have strong propensities toward saving, if producers have pessimistic expectations and hence low incentives toward investment, and if there is a strong liquidity preference generally, equilibrium national income may involve massive unemployment throughout the economy.

[8] To understand this point, it is necessary to notice that a low interest rate implies, in the case of a bond, a high purchase price. When we say that interest rates are very low, we are saying, in effect, that bond prices are very high. Keynes argued that when bond prices were very high, people would anticipate a fall in their prices (a rise in the interest-rate) and would be very hesitant to buy them. They would prefer to hold on to "liquid" money.

Such, in the fewest possible words, was Keynes' central analytic contribution to modern economics.[9]

THE ECONOMIC CONSEQUENCES
OF LORD KEYNES

But what remains of all this now, three decades after the *General Theory* was published? How much of the contribution was permanent? As in the case of Marx, it will be convenient to separate the analytic developments stemming from Keynes' work from the somewhat broader questions of social philosophy and public policy.

Post-Keynesian Macro-economics

Although we have pointed out (and critics have stressed) that Keynes had been anticipated by other theorists on many of his important points, the actual impact of the *General Theory* on the evolution of modern economics was immediate and dramatic. Not least was the impact on the critics themselves, for, faced with a demand for a general reconstruction of economics, they were forced to re-write traditional theory in ways that could stand up against the Keynesian assault. In so doing, they improved that theory enormously, making it far more realistic and cogent than it has ever been before.

More generally, Keynesian ideas gave a great stimulus to the further development of macro-economics. For one thing, there was a need to refine the tools which Keynes himself had used, many of which were no better than first approximations. Consider, for example, the relationship between consumption and its determinants, a crucial matter in Keynesian theory. Keynes, as we have seen, spoke of a "fundamental psychological law" relating consumption to income, but this "law" was actually a very rough empirical generalization. In the last thirty years there has been an enormous amount of research and theorizing about what is now called the *consumption function*. One hypothesis—suggested by the eminent British economist, A. C. Pigou, whose work had been treated critically in the *General Theory*—was that Keynes had erred in making consumption solely a function of income and in neglecting the influence of a consumer's stock of wealth on his consumption decision. The so-called "Pigou effect" suggested theoretical reasons why consumption might rise with respect to income when prices were falling and also helped explain why consumption after World War II in countries like the United States was so high relative to income.[10]

[9] A full exposition of the Keynesian system would take a book in itself; indeed, it has already taken several such. In this series, the central ideas of the Keynesian analysis, as they appear in modern form, are given in Charles L. Schultze, *National Income Analysis*, 2nd ed., and James S. Duesenberry, *Money and Credit: Impact and Control*, 2nd ed.

[10] Wealth is a *stock* concept; whereas income is a *flow* concept. Suppose the stock of money is fixed but that money wages and prices are falling in an economy.

Another idea—on the same general subject—pointed out the interdependence of consumption decisions as among different consumers (shades of Veblen!). Such American economists as James Duesenberry argued that a consumer's desire to purchase goods would be positively affected by the purchases of other consumers, with the result that consumption, as a percentage of income, might depend not on a person's absolute level of income but on his *relative* position in the over-all income distribution. Duesenberry also suggested that consumption levels in one period might be positively affected by a previously achieved higher level of income—that is, that consumers would be resistant to downward adjustments in consumption when income was falling.

More recently, Milton Friedman, the University of Chicago economist and a well-known and articulate spokesman for "conservative" economic policies, has brought forth still another theory of the consumption function. He divides a consumer's income into a "permanent income" element and a "transitory income" element and argues that consumption is mainly a function of "permanent income." This is consistent with the notion that savings are a "residual" and that windfall gains or losses are more likely to lead to changes in accumulated balances and holdings of durable goods than to changes in ordinary consumption.[11] The analysis has thus become increasingly refined and complex as economists have moved away from the simple Keynesian formulations to a more adequate confrontation with economic realities.

But Keynesian economics needed more than refinement—it also needed extended foundations. One of its most glaring weaknesses was in the area of economic growth. Keynes' analysis is strictly relevant only to a relatively short period of time and, indeed, his whole interest was in short-run analysis and short-run policy measures.[12]

The result was that, within a few years of its publication, economists everywhere were engaged in the effort to re-write the *General Theory* in long-run dynamic terms. One of the most interesting attempts in this direction was R. F. Harrod's *Towards a Dynamic Economics* (1949). Harrod pointed out the obvious fact that Keynes' treatment of investment was one-sided.

This will mean that the *real* value of the stock of money wealth is increasing. Pigou argued that, having more real wealth, people would increase their consumption from a given income. At the end of World War II, many people had extraordinary holdings of wealth in the form of government savings bonds and this fact undoubtedly contributed to their relatively high consumption from income—and consequently the failure of the expected serious post-War depression to materialize.

[11] See Milton Friedman, *A Theory of the Consumption Function* (Princeton: Princeton University Press, 1957). The reader is warned, however, that this is a highly technical book, rather unlike Friedman's more expansive ventures such as *Capitalism and Freedom* (Chicago: University of Chicago Press, 1962).

[12] Keynes' attitude to long-run problems was indicated by his succinct comment: "In the long run we are all dead." But, of course, the Great Depression was a short-run, crisis problem! Reflections on the long-run seemed at the time a luxury not to be afforded.

While Keynes laid emphasis on the role of investment in creating a demand for goods (and hence more employment), he had purposely ignored the fact that investment represents an addition to the stock of capital goods of the economy (and hence to long-run productive capacity). What Harrod (and others, such at MIT's Evsey Domar) attempted was to see what happened when the stock of capital, population, and technology were all expanding over time. Although many additional steps have been taken since that time, the Harrod-Domar formulations were enormously stimulating attempts to bring growth back into economics while still taking advantage of the Keynesian advances.

In short, from the point of view of economic *analysis,* Keynesian economics has been modified, improved, and extended since it was first presented to the world. There is almost nothing from the *General Theory* that remains today exactly as it was then. As a source of stimulation to both theoretical and empirical research, however, the book has had no equal in twentieth-century economics. In this respect, the term "new economics" does not seem too much of an exaggeration.

Policies, Remedies, and Social Philosophy

Keynesian economics was not simply analysis, however; it was also social philosophy and public policy. It is time now to say a word about this aspect of the matter.

In a fundamental sense, Keynes broke with earlier *laissez-faire* ideas because he believed that there was no guarantee that a market economy would generate sufficient aggregate demand to maintain full employment. More specifically, he feared that there would be a tendency in advanced capitalistic countries for the incentives to saving to outrun the incentives for investment. To prevent general unemployment, the State would have to intervene.

He saw this intervention as occurring in two general ways. *One* way of stimulating private investment would be to take steps to keep the rate of interest low. Keynes argued that interest payments no longer served any useful social purpose and, indeed, by posing obstacles in investment, could be a contributing cause of depressions. He thus anticipated a gradual lowering of interest rates and, with it, the decline of the social class that depends heavily on interest. A *second,* and perhaps more significant, way for the State to help prevent depressions was by taking a direct role in affecting consumer and investment expenditures. By its tax policies the government could directly alter the take-home pay of consumers and influence their consumption patterns; it could also influence corporate income and spending. Moreover, the government could participate directly in investment activities as a supplement to private enterprise. Keynes foresaw a certain "socialization of investment." The government, he argued, should take the responsibility for insuring that there was no general deficiency of aggregate demand in the economy. In 99 order to do this, its spending on socially useful investments might have to be increased.

How far these new functions of government would have to be carried, Keynes did not definitely predict. While the *direction* of change was clear to him, the *extent* of change that would be necessary would depend on how conditions developed in the future. It is interesting to note, however, that he did not believe that the changed role of the government would lead to a comprehensive socialization of the economy as a whole. Nor did he desire such a socialization. For Keynes believed that individualism was important as the safeguard of personal liberty, of the variety of life, and, indeed, of economic efficiency. His basic social objective was to find ways of correcting capitalistic society, not of overthrowing it, and, in this sense, he was the very opposite of Marx, and his philosophy a major alternative to Marxism.[13]

The immediate effect of Keynesian doctrine (and also, of course, of the Great Depression itself!) was a good deal of pessimism about the future of mature capitalistic societies. In the late 'thirties and early 'forties, there developed a school of American economists called the "stagnationists," of which the distinguished economist Alvin Hansen was one of the leading exponents. Hansen argued that full employment (or near full employment) had been achieved in nineteenth-century America for a variety of special reasons such as our rapid population growth and the existence of our undeveloped frontier. But in the twentieth century these factors favoring high levels of investment were no longer so vigorous. Consequently, there was a danger that investment would fall short of saving and unemployment would result, unless the State intervened on Keynesian lines.

In the more buoyant conditions of the post-World War II world, the "stagnationist" predictions appear to have been somewhat pessimistic.[14] In a more basic sense, however, Keynes and his followers left behind a permanent legacy in the form of a new view of the role of the State in modern economic life. In late nineteenth-century analysis, the State does not appear explicitly in the analysis. The theory is that of a private market economy; the effect of this or that government action may be analyzed, but fundamentally the focus

[13] Since Keynes' purposes were so different from those of Marx, it will not come as a surprise that he had a rather low opinion of Marxian economics. In the letter to George Bernard Shaw previously mentioned, he disposes of Marx and Engels with the following: "I can see that they invented a certain method of carrying on and a vile manner of writing, both of which their successors have maintained with fidelity. But if you tell me that they discovered a clue to the economic riddle, still I am beaten—I can discover nothing but out-of-date controversialising." In the *General Theory*, Keynes admitted that Marx had had some inkling of the unemployment problem, but he thought that the future had more to learn from a virtually unknown economist (Silvio Gesell) than from Marx.

[14] Though it can be said in their defense that the State has in fact become much more active in our economic life than was the case in the 1920's and 1930's. And undoubtedly this *has* been a factor in keeping employment generally high during the past two decades. For a description of the growth of government in the American economy, see, in this Series, Otto Eckstein, *Public Finance,* esp. Ch. 1.

is on a private system. In the Keynesian world, however, the State appears immediately as an intrinsic factor in the life of the economy. It does so because its actions—whatever the intentions behind them—necessarily and directly affect the society's total demand for goods and services and thus the over-all level of output and employment.

Once this effect is clearly recognized, it is inevitable to ask whether the activities the government is engaged in are favorable, unfavorable, or neutral with respect to the economy as a whole. Are the activities of government, in their total impact, expansionary or contractionary? Are they making a depressed situation worse, aggravating an inflation? One begins to think of the economy not as a purely private economy in which the government occasionally intervenes, but as a "mixed economy" in which the existence of government and the nature of its effects must be explicitly analyzed.

This change in view has affected not only economists but also the actions of governments themselves. In most industrial countries of the Western world at the present time, national governments are acutely aware that when they expand or contract expenditures or taxes or both they are directly affecting the potential prosperity of their economies. The United States has been one of the more conservative countries in this respect, but the tax cut of 1964, which reduced tax liabilities by over $10 billion, gave clear evidence that this country now accepts much of the new philosophy. For this tax cut did not come about because, along traditional lines, the government was cutting expenditures or was accumulating a surplus of revenues. On the contrary, the *main* impetus behind it was the view that a cut in taxes, in the particular circumstances of the nation at that time, would favorably affect the prosperity of the economy as a whole. And this kind of thinking is, in essence, Keynesian.

The impact of his ideas about the role of the State is thus a tribute to Keynes' influence not only on economists but also on the actual course of affairs. It is also a vindication of his view of history. For, as he said in one of his most-quoted passages: "Soon or late, it is ideas, not vested interests, which are dangerous for good or evil." He had a great faith in the capacity of men for rational action, and, indeed, it was this faith that made him believe capitalism could survive despite its defects. Once men had a "right analysis of the problem," he thought it likely that they would be able to "cure the disease whilst preserving efficiency and freedom."

And so far, it should be said, there has been no good reason to doubt the wisdom of that prediction.

SUMMARY

Keynesian economics was born in the Great Depression of the 1930's although there had been many anticipations, dating back to the mercantilists, and including the work of the Swedish economist, Wicksell. **101**

Keynes' *General Theory* (1936) continued the traditions of mainstream economics in many respects but departed from them in that: (1) its main focus was on macro-economics rather than micro-economics; (2) it greatly emphasized aggregate demand and its components—consumption, investment and government demand; (3) it argued for the possibility of underemployment equilibrium; (4) it attempted to unify monetary and real economics in a novel way; and (5) it urged, in the absence of effective market guarantees, the intervention of the State to maintain full employment.

The Keynesian system showed that, in a private economy, aggregate demand (consumption demand plus investment demand) might fall short at full employment income. Consumption demand (and consequently savings) was a function of national income. Investment demand depended on business expectations and the rate of interest. The rate of interest, in turn, was influenced by the amount of money in the economy and people's liquidity preferences. The likelihood of mass unemployment was increased by: an increase in the propensity to save (a decrease in the propensity to consume), more pessimistic business expectations, and any factor tending to raise the rate of interest, such as increased liquidity preference or a decrease in the quantity of money.

The legacy of Keynesian economics was substantial both in terms of economic theory and economic policy. The decades following the *General Theory* have seen an enormous amount of theoretical and empirical research designed to test, modify, and expand hypotheses presented or suggested by Keynes' work. In policy terms, the main effect of Keynesian doctrine has been to make both scholars and nations aware that governmental tax and expenditure policies can, and do, have substantial effects on the over-all health of the economy. In consequence, most Western nations—now including the United States—think of fiscal policy as an important tool in correcting either unemployment or inflation.

Keynes himself believed that such measures would preserve the basic features of capitalistic society, and the successes of the "mixed economies" of the post-World War II period suggest that his optimism was justified.

Postscript: Currents

in Contemporary Economics

In this postscript, we shall sketch a few trends in present-day economics that are likely to shape its future evolution. These trends all have roots in the past, but the speed of change today is very rapid. We live in the age of the "knowledge explosion." Economics has become a complex discipline that attempts to reach an ever wider range of problems with increasingly sophisticated techniques.

STATISTICS, MATHEMATICS, ECONOMETRICS

A postscript about these latest developments should point out first of all the enormous growth of factual and especially statistical knowledge about economic problems. The pioneering efforts of Sir William Petty in the seventeenth century to deal in "Number, Weight, or Measure" have now borne fruit. In the mid-twentieth century, statistics come from literally hundreds of sources: national agencies (such as our Department of Commerce and Bureau of Labor Statistics), international organizations (such as the United Nations and International Monetary Fund), private scholars and research foundations (such as our National Bureau of Economic Research (NBER)). The collection and evaluation of these data have required not only enormous labor but also a much more refined conceptual apparatus. Men like Simon Kuznets, for-

103

merly of the University of Pennsylvania and Johns Hopkins and now of Harvard, have devoted their lives to such problems. Kuznets' work on national income statistics for the NBER gave empirical life to Keynesian macroeconomics and provided an independent stimulation to work on aggregative economic problems. Kuznets has also helped lay the empirical basis for the modern interest in growth in developed and underdeveloped countries.[1]

Besides the growth of economic statistics, our postscript should point up certain general changes in the methods of economics. The increasing information available to economists has been matched by an increasing sophistication of theoretical technique. The student who picks up a present-day economic journal will see immediately what is meant. Indeed, he is very likely to decide that Walras (who blatantly praised mathematical economics) was far more prophetic than Marshall (who hid his mathematics in his appendices). Mathematical economics is now the order of the day in most branches of theoretical economics. Economists like MIT's Paul Samuelson have proved the desirability and even necessity of mathematical techniques for important ranges of economic problems. Samuelson's *Foundations of Economic Analysis* (1947) was an outstanding effort to re-write much of traditional economic theory into mathematical terms and to extend that theory into new areas such as that of economic dynamics. Except for the more institutional branches of economics (labor economics, economic history, and the like), the victory of the mathematical economist is virtually complete today; or, to put it more accurately, every economist at the present time finds is necessary to know at least some mathematics for use in his professional work.

Perhaps the most novel feature of current economic method, however, is neither its statistical collections nor its mathematical techniques taken alone, but precisely the attempt to join the statistical and the theoretical together. *Econometrics* is the art of formulating economic theories in mathematical form and subjecting them to quantitative empirical testing. Many present-day economists are extremely enthusiastic about the potentialities of such econometric model-building; others are more reserved; but all recognize the need for continuing research in this area since it is perfectly clear that fact-without-theory and theory-without-fact are equally useless and since it is also clear that much of the basic material of economics (unlike some other social sciences) comes in essentially quantitative form. All that econometrics does is to try to take cognizance of these facts in a systematic way.

In a deeper sense, the modern emphasis on statistics and econometrics is a continuation of the trend toward greater realism in economics that we noted in the two preceding chapters. Economists have become increasingly impressed by the need for fleshing out their theoretical constructs with real

[1] For Kuznets' early work see such NBER publications as his *National Income and Capital Formation, 1919-1935* (1937) and *National Income, A Summary of Findings* (1946). Some of his more recent work on economic development is summed up in *Six Lectures on Economic Growth* (New York: The Free Press of Glencoe, 1959).

life numbers. Attempts to do this, as, for example, Professor Leontief's *input-output analysis,* have shown that success is possible. Input-output analysis is a distant heir of the *Tableau Économique* of the physiocrats and the general equilibrium analysis of the late-nineteenth century. The difference is that it represents an elaborate modern attempt to put actual, as opposed to hypothetical, quantities into the general equilibrium framework. As Leontief describes it simply, it is "an attempt to apply the economic theory of general equilibrium . . . to an empirical study of interrelations among the different parts of a national economy." The input-output table of the American economy includes hundreds of industries showing how the output of each industry is broken down into inputs into all the other industries of the economy. The ultimate purpose of all this is to show what happens when there are changes in the allocation of a society's productive efforts—as, for example, an increased defense effort. The table enables one to trace through the total impact, direct and indirect, of such changes on the economy. Thus, input-output analysis is very useful for the economic planner, and Professor Leontief's achievements have been paid the high compliment of emulation by Russia and other Iron Curtain countries.[2]

GROWTH ECONOMICS

The above changes are largely changes in method, but we must also mention certain changes in subject matter.

The Keynesian Revolution has, of course, been a continuing stimulus to the expansion of the traditional boundaries of economics. The rapid development of macro-economics, which we have already touched on and which presses onward at the present time, must rank as one of the important trends in contemporary economics. This development bids fair to make the business cycle—at least in its grosser and more injurious forms—a thing of the past. If this prediction holds, then it will mean that economics has to its credit an achievement that few other social sciences can claim: a set of therapeutic measures of importance and relevance to a major social ill! Indeed, from a practical (as opposed to theoretical) point of view, this may represent the most significant single achievement of mid-twentieth century social science.

However, economics has pushed well past the Keynesian range of considerations. Indeed, if one wished to sum up the central interest of contemporary economic analysis in a phrase, it would probably have to be *economic growth.* Again, this is a development with strong roots in the past. R. F. Harrod, whose interest in growth we have mentioned, indicated that he had a debt not only to Keynes but even more significantly to Ricardo! Indeed, in certain fields of modern growth analysis, Ricardian and Malthusian and

[2] For a basic work on input-output analysis, see Wassily W. Leontief, *Structure of the American Economy, 1919-1939* (New York: Oxford University Press, 1951).

even certain Marxian concepts have proved extremely helpful.[3] And, of course, it is only in recent years that Schumpeter has begun to come into his own.

Modern growth analysis has, however, penetrated far beyond the range of these beginnings and, in several of its branches, it can really be described as a new field. There is—to give a few examples—the theory of *optimum growth,* a field opened up by a brilliant young British mathematical economist, Frank Ramsey, in the 1920's and by John von Neumann in the mid-1930's. In this field, which is currently attracting some of the best theoretical economists, the problem is to take certain long-run objectives for an economy (e.g. maximizing the capital stock of the economy at some specified future date) and then to determine the optimum growth path the economy should take to fulfill this objective. This is clearly very abstract analysis; the methods used are wholly mathematical.

Another, quite different, growth field is concerned with the attempt to weigh the various causal factors that make for rapid growth in the real world. This field might almost be called the analysis of the *residual,* since the investigations of Edward F. Denison, Robert M. Solow, and others have shown that relatively little of, say, twentieth-century American growth can be accounted for by changes in capital and labor supply—a great deal is left over to be explained by a "residual" item called "technical progress." Consequently, very extensive research is now being undertaken in such areas as the influence of education on economic growth and the nature and impact of invention and technological change.

Still another growth field, and one which has attracted great attention in the past fifteen years, is that of the *underdeveloped economies.* The problem of poor countries is not a new one in the world's history, but it is only quite recently that economists in the Western world have paid heed to it in a serious way. The literature of economic development is characteristically very different from that of, say, optimum growth theory. It is filled with case studies of particular countries and particular problems; it takes up broad questions that involve not only economics but history, political science, sociology, even anthropology; it is very heavily oriented toward policy decision-making problems. Still, like the other fields we have mentioned, it shares a concern about the nature and causes of economic expansion over time and thus is another example of the contemporary emphasis on growth.

The combined impact of modern growth economics and the earlier developments in national income analysis has extended considerably the range of economics during the past 20 years or so. There was a time in the late-nineteenth century when economic analysis seemed likely to become confined almost wholly to static competitive general equilibrium theory. We have

[3] This is particularly true of the analysis of underdeveloped countries. See, for example, W. A. Lewis' article, "Economic Development with Unlimited Supplies of Labour," *Manchester School,* May 1954, an influential modern growth article which takes classical-Marxian concepts as a starting point.

seen how a series of steps—the introduction of the theories of imperfect competition, the Keynesian Revolution, the great current interest in growth—have steadily expanded the boundaries of the field and especially that part of the field that is susceptible to systematic analysis. Anyone who looks at the newer areas will realize how very much still remains to be done within them. (A good example is the problem of the *residual* which has been described as a "measure of our ignorance" of the causes of economic growth.) Still, the initial explorations are being made and past experience suggests that progress is not beyond reach.

THE ISSUES OF THE FUTURE

But what of the future? Are the questions currently occupying economists likely to be the urgent questions of the next half century? Or are there new questions already foreseeable on the horizon?

The answer must necessarily be rather speculative. Certainly many of the questions economists are trying to analyze today will be with us for a long time to come. A good example is the problem of economic development. Experience in the past two decades has made it abundantly clear that the development of the poor countries of the world is a complex, arduous, and difficult-to-understand process. We can expect increasing attention to such problems as population control, agricultural development, industrialization and urbanization, and foreign aid. In due course (hopefully) the under-development problem will disappear; but in the next half century it is bound to remain a major public issue requiring continuing theoretical and empirical study.

At the same time, however, it does seem possible to anticipate certain rather new centers of interest for the economists of the future. Already there are signs of stirring with respect to what we might call *beyond economic growth* issues. The problem may be put this way: For the past century or two the advanced industrial economies have been growing at unprecedentedly rapid rates, creating unprecedented riches for their citizens. In such societies, it may possibly be the case that economic growth is no longer the fundamental question. Much more serious may be some of the problems that arise in the world that growth has created: the world of luxury, leisure, and longevity.

The book that brought this range of problems to the fore was, more than any other, *The Affluent Society* (1958) by John Kenneth Galbraith, Harvard professor, friend to President Kennedy, and former ambassador to India. The term "affluent society" is a curious one for an economist to use because economics has traditionally been concerned with the problem of "scarcity." But this is precisely Galbraith's point—that traditional ideas are inadequate because the problem has changed from scarcity to affluence. Failing to adjust to our new circumstances, he claims, we find ourselves "guided, in part, by **107** ideas that are relevant to another world" and doing "many things that are unnecessary, some that are unwise, and a few that are insane."

In Galbraith's view the affluent society requires rather less attention to the increasing production of private goods (economic growth) and rather more to certain public needs (education, urban development, parks) which a privately oriented growth process is likely to ignore. Thus his argument becomes a modern addition to the great historical debate about State intervention versus *laissez-faire* and the proper balance of public and private interests.

Our concern here, however, is not with this part of his argument—on which, of course, many economists would differ from him—but rather with the opening up of a new *range* of economic issues. And here he is on indisputable ground. For attitudes and theoretical constructs created in an age when poverty was the general rule seem unlikely to be ideal in an age when poverty is the exception (though an important exception)[4] and most people find themselves relatively at ease. Thus, to take a very simple example, the problem of leisure time and our attitude to work as opposed to relaxation is almost certain to be wholly different in a society where everyone is working long, back-breaking hours each day as compared to a society where the work week is short, retirement often comes early, and leisure time is a definite problem to be coped with in one way or another.

More generally, it seems possible to argue that the well-to-do, economically advanced society may find itself less concerned with the problems of mass production (so handsomely solved by modern technology) than with the problems of what has been called the "quality of life." The preservation of our natural heritage, the renewal of our tarnished cities, the cultural development of our citizens young and old—these issues, which are already part of the political program of the Great Society, have a rather different flavor from the bread-and-butter issues of economics in the past.

Of course, it might be objected that in shifting from scarcity to affluence we would be not so much shifting positions within economics as going beyond the boundaries of economics altogether. Would there be a fundamental need for the discipline of economics in a society in which the problem of scarcity had been solved? Is it not possible that economists, who have often discussed technological unemployment in other fields, may themselves ultimately become the victim of it?

And, of course, this may be what eventually happens, though it still seems a long way off and there is no reason to think that economists would not simply focus on slightly different aspects of society's problems. What all

[4] Interestingly, the recent discovery of "poverty" in the United States has gone hand in hand with the discovery of our "affluence." Galbraith, for example, speaks of the "new position of poverty": it is no longer general poverty we have to worry about but *case poverty* (the handicapped, the disadvantaged) and *insular poverty* (Appalachia). Indeed, this new view of poverty is a characteristic example of how, according to Galbraith, we must re-think standard economic problems in the affluent society.

this does bring out, however, is that the evolution of modern economics that we have been tracing in these pages is a continuing, on-going process. The achievements of that evolution to date are substantial. In the two centuries of its modern existence, economics has reached for the abstract and theoretical but has also confronted the concrete and practical. The applied mathematician can make his home here; but so also can the senator and ordinary citizen. In the future the field will almost certainly continue to become more professional and complex in its methods. As we said at the very outset, economics has developed cumulatively over time and consequently the level of analysis has deepened with each generation. But this has been only part of the story. And the remaining part—the controversy, the difference of opinion, the various concepts of what society is or should be—has been no less significant. The future course of the field will be guided by the disciplined professional but it will also be influenced by the man who has what Schumpeter called "vision"—a new view of old facts, an unconventional way of ordering the commonplaces of our everyday existence.

The subject of this book—the evolution of modern economics—covers potentially the whole body of economic literature of the past two centuries or more. Every interested student should clearly examine at firsthand the major classics we have discussed. Adam Smith's *Wealth of Nations,* Malthus' *Essay on Population,* Ricardo's *Principles of Political Economy and Taxation,* John Stuart Mill's *Principles of Political Economy,* Marx's *Capital* and *Communist Manifesto,* Marshall's *Principles of Economics,* Veblen's *Theory of the Leisure Class,* Schumpeter's *Theory of Economic Development,* Chamberlin's *Theory of Monopolistic Competition,* Keynes' *General Theory of Employment, Interest, and Money,* Galbraith's *Affluent Society*—these, and the many other books we have discussed, form the core of the subject at hand and there is ultimately no substitute for reading them directly.

These various works differ greatly in length and difficulty, however, and it is useful to have one or more guides through economic literature generally and through individual books specifically. The best and most comprehensive, but also definitely flawed, general work on the evolution of economics is, in the author's opinion, Joseph A. Schumpeter's *History of Economic Analysis* (New York: Oxford University Press, 1954). This work suffers from disorganization (it was published after Schumpeter's death), length (1,260 pages), and temperament (he is hard on Adam Smith, antagonistic to Ricardo, and condescending to Keynes). But the book is written by a master economist and this more than outweighs its evident defects.

Other books dealing with the general evolution of economics include: O. H. Taylor, *A History of Economic Thought* (New York: McGraw-Hill, 1960), a recently published but traditional account of the development of political economy; George J. Stigler, *Essays in the History of Economics* (Chicago: University of Chicago Press, 1964), excellent essays on a variety of subjects including Ricardo, J. S. Mill, and utility theory; Robert L. Heilbroner, *The Worldly Philosophers* (New York: Simon and Schuster,

1961), a popular and highly readable account of the theories and lives, and especially lives, of the great economists; J. M. Keynes, *Essays in Biography* (New York: Harcourt, Brace, 1933), especially notable for the essay on Marshall; Philip Newman, Arthur Gayer and Milton Spencer, eds., *Source Readings in Economic Thought* (New York: Norton, 1954), a collection of readings from Aristotle to the present with very brief introductory notices; and Philip Newman, *The Development of Economic Thought* (Englewood Cliffs, N.J.: Prentice-Hall, 1952), an account dedicated to, and bearing much of the influence of, Wesley Mitchell. In addition, there are several histories of economic thought that have been around for some years and still have worthwhile material in them, such as, Eric Roll, *A History of Economic Thought*, 3rd ed. (Englewood Cliffs, N.J.: Prentice-Hall, 1953) and Gide and Rist, *A History of Economic Doctrines* (London: G. G. Hamp, 1948).

For guidance through the Marxian maze, see Paul Sweezy, *Theory of Capitalist Development* (New York: Oxford University Press, 1942)—a partial but intelligent account—and also Schumpeter's, *Capitalism, Socialism and Democracy* (New York: Harper, 1947)—the first part of which is an essay on Marx. For guidance through the rigors of Keynesian analysis, see Alvin Hansen, *A Guide to Keynes* (New York: McGraw-Hill, 1953). Hansen's *Business Cycles and National Income* (New York: Norton, 1951) also includes (Part III) a long summary of the history of modern business cycle theory. For a guide, not easy however, to the complexities of modern growth theory, see John Hicks, *Capital and Growth* (Oxford: Oxford University Press, 1965).

Index

115